ASTON MARTIN

THE GREAT BRITISH INSTITUTION

igloobooks

igloobooks

Published in 2013
by Igloo Books Ltd
Cottage Farm
Sywell
NN6 0BJ
www.igloobooks.com

FIR003 1013
2 4 6 8 10 9 7 5 3 1
ISBN 978-1-78343-205-9

Distributed in association with G2 Entertainment Limited

Printed and manufactured in China

Contents

Introduction

▲ The famous Aston Martin winged badge

ASTON MARTIN – THOSE TWO SIMPLE words conquer up exciting images in any car enthusiast's mind. Images of power, speed and elegance with a dash of suavity thrown in.

Above all, perhaps, Aston Martin conveys an image of Britishness. Ask anyone to name a British high-performance car, and Aston Martin should be top of their list.

As with most British marques, Aston Martin has had more than its fair share of troubles over the years; usually financial. However, against all odds, has survived and evolved over the years to be the respected brand it is today.

Many other British car manufacturers have either gone by the wayside, or their brand values have become diluted. Lotus, TVR, Jaguar and even Rolls Royce all have negative connotations today, but not so Aston Martin.

Aston Martin has managed to retain its aura of exclusivity, and owning one shows that you have impeccable taste and appreciate the best things in life.

This little book gives a potted history of Aston Martin, outlining the company's chequered background and how has evolved to be the prestige marque it

is today, recognised around the world.

It also features some of the most interesting and important road-going models that Aston Martin has produced over the years. Space prohibits putting them all in, but you'll find a representative cross-section of mouth-watering machines.

There is also, of course, a section on James Bond, who has undoubtedly done wonders for Aston Martin's image over the years. But don't let the James Bond connection flavour your view of the marque; even without 007, an Aston Martin would still be a very cool car to own.

▲ Exclusivity has always been a figure of the Aston Martin marque

Chapter 1

A brief history of Aston Martin

Bamford & Martin

IT'S FUNNY TO THINK THAT, IF history had turned out just a little differently, the badge on the front of these most British of cars could have read 'Bamford Martin'. You see, the company which started on 15 January 1913 was called Bamford & Martin, after its two founders, Robert Bamford and Lionel Martin.

Bamford was born in 1883, the son of a clergyman, and a talented engineer. Martin, on the other hand, was born in 1878 to a wealthy mining family and grew up to be an enthusiastic driver, competing in hillclimbs and trials.

The two had met at a cycling club in 1905 and soon became firm friends. Their original company was based in West London, just off the Fulham Road, and sold Singer cars. Before long, as well as the standard models, the two entrepreneurs were offering tuned versions with a claimed top speed of 70mph – a worthwhile improvement over the standard 45mph. Naturally, they were using these modified cars in competition themselves.

Before long, though, Bamford and Martin had dreams of producing their own cars – ones that offered better performance and quality than the trusty Singers. They moved to larger premises in West Kensington and, before they'd

even produced a car, they'd come up with a name. Lionel Martin had had some modest success on the Aston Clinton hillclimb in the Chiltons, so it was decided that the new venture would be christened 'Aston Martin'. And so a legend was born.

The first car to bear the Aston Martin name was built in 1915. It was a two-seater racing car powered by a modified 1389cc side-valve Coventry-Simplex engine. Very much a prototype, this car was soon nicknamed the 'Coal Scuttle' and Martin put it into service

ABOVE Count Louis Zborowski, winner of the Gold Vase at Brooklands. He became better known as the designer of the famous aero-engined Chitty Chitty Bang Bang

▲ The vehicle used in the stage musical Chitty Chitty Bang Bang

competing in hillclimbs and other events around the UK.

Sadly, though, the First World War put a stop to any further development and it was not until 1920 that a second prototype was built, this time with a 1487cc engine. Soon after, Bamford left the company, leaving Lionel Martin in charge. Martin did, though, have financial backing from an old school friend, Count Louis Zborowski. Zborowski was of Polish-American descent and was himself a keen racing driver and engineer. In fact, he'd already produced an outrageous, 23-litre car that had been christened 'Chitty Bang Bang' on account of the sound that the massive aero engine produced. Years later, Ian Fleming would base his children's book, Chitty Chitty Bang Bang, on the car (by a happy coincidence, Fleming also created the James Bond character who, famously, would drive Aston Martins).

In 1922, Zborowski himself drove an early Aston Martin – nicknamed

'Bunny' – at Brooklands, averaging a speed of 76mph and breaking no less than 10 world records in just 16.5 hours. In the same year, Aston Martins competed in the French Grand Prix and so the marque became a household name in the UK.

It was an exciting time and should have been a successful one, too, but it wasn't. Lionel Martin was struggling to make ends meet because he only sold around 50 cars over two years which, despite each one costing over £700 (a huge amount of money in those days), it was simply not enough.

Another investor, Lady Charnwood, stepped in and her son, John Benson, worked with Martin to attempt to turn the company around. It didn't work out, though, and they went into receivership in 1925, with Martin walking out for good. He returned to working with bicycles and, tragically, was killed in a biking accident in 1945.

▲ Motor racing at Brooklands with Lionel Martin in the centre in an Aston Martin

ABOVE LEFT An Aston Martin being admired by fans at Brooklands in 1923

Aston Martin Motors

THE CHARNWOOD FAMILY THEN relaunched the company a year later, renaming it Aston Martin Motors and bringing on board a Birmingham-based engineering company, Renwick & Bertelli. William Renwick and Domenico Augustus Bertelli had recently gone into business with the aim of building the best car in the world, so the idea of a tie-up with the already known Aston Martin marque was appealing.

The new company moved to the former Citroën plant in Feltham, West London, and Bertelli – known affectionately as 'Our Bert' – threw himself into developing cars. Bertelli proved to be, not only a talented driver and engineer, but also knew how to run a company.

Renwick & Bertelli had already developed a sophisticated 1.5-litre overhead-cam engine and this unit was used as the basis of the new cars, in place of the less reliable side-valve powerplant. Meanwhile, Bertelli's brother, Harry, produced the bodyshells.

◀ A 1926 Renwick-Bertelli which was the prototype for the Aston Martin and reached speeds of up to 85mph

▲The 11-9 hp Le Mans Sports Model of 1931

The key model at this stage was the Aston Martin International, which was proving to be an exceptional race and road car, and Bertelli put into place a busy racing programme to promote the marque. In 1928, an Aston Martin made its first appearance at the Le Mans 24-Hour race; an event at which the company would go on to become regular competitors. Indeed, the cars' reliability proved a great asset on this and other endurance events.

The problem with all this competition was that it cost a lot of money and, despite Bertelli's best efforts, Aston Martin was still not financially secure and ended up badly in debt. In 1932, therefore, it was taken over by a new

investor, Sir Arthur Sutherland, who made his son, Gordon, managing director. They had big plans for Aston Martin and cut back on the motorsport spending to concentrate on developing new models. First up was the Le Mans, which replaced the International and then, in 1934, came the Mark II and the Ulster. These cars offered more comfort and sophistication than did previous Aston Martins.

Up until now, all Aston Martins had been powered by the trusty Renwick & Bertelli 1.5-litre engine, but Sutherland put into place the development of a larger, 2.0-litre engine. This first appeared in the Aston Martin 15/98 of 1935.

The following year, Bertelli left the company, because he found it difficult working with Gordon Sutherland; Renwick had already left. This left Aston Martin somewhat directionless for a while before Sutherland decided to change tack and develop a futuristic road car, designed by Claude Hill, a draughtsman who had been with the company since Bertelli joined. The result was the Atom concept car, a streamlined coupe which was way ahead of its time, with its tubular chassis and electric gearbox.

Unfortunately, though, the Second World War restricted the development of the startling Atom, although the devoted Hill continued to tinker with it throughout hostilities while the factory was put to work making aircraft parts for nearby Vickers.

David Brown

ONCE THE WAR WAS OVER, THE Sutherlands decided they'd had enough and, in 1946, the Aston Martin company was anonymously and quietly advertised for sale in the classified advertisements of The Times newspaper, with an asking price of £30,000, claiming that the net profits for the previous year had been £4000.

The advertisement for 'A high-class motor business' was spotted by Yorkshireman, David Brown, who was managing director of the long-established David Brown Group engineering concern which produced, among other things, tractors and gears.

Brown was an enthusiastic racing driver and so was intrigued by the notice. He got in touch and travelled to Feltham to see what was on offer. As it was, there was very little – an old workshop, some tools, an engine or two and an odd-looking, rather rusty car – the Atom. Brown chatted with Claude Hill who agreed to lend him the Atom for a few days. He drove the prototype home to Huddersfield and was suitably impressed by its handling, although he found the 1970cc engine disappointing.

It was, though, enough to persuade him that Aston Martin was worth buying and, in February 1947, Brown wrote a cheque for £20,500 of his own money to purchase the company name and its few assets. He also kept the talented

◀ The Spa replica

Claude Hill and Gordon Sutherland on the management board. The same year, Brown acquired the Lagonda company (for a hefty £52,500) which had built large, expensive motorcars before the war and was based in Staines.

This gave Brown the engineering abilities of Claude Hill combined with the styling skills of Lagonda's Frank Feeley, not to mention a six-cylinder engine designed by William Bentley. Hill and Feeley worked together on a

new car and the result was the astonishingly fresh-looking Aston Martin 2-litre of 1948, which later unofficially became referred to as the 'DB1'.

That same year, Aston Martin began racing again – Brown understood the importance of good publicity – and a car known as the Aston Martin Spa Special won the Spa 24-Hour race. The future was looking good for David Brown's new purchase.

Indeed, he was so pleased that he added his own name to the company's next car, thus beginning a long tradition. Not only was the 1950 model badged 'DB2', the name 'David Brown' was added to the winged Aston Martin bonnet badge. And who can blame him for wanting to do so? The Feeley-designed DB2

◀ David Brown, head of the David Brown Corporation which makes luxury cars and agricultural machinery, introduces the new Lagonda, which reaches speeds of up to 170mph, 22nd April 1954

OPPOSITE A 1953 Aston Martin

with its 2.6-litre Lagonda engine really was a thing of beauty and set the standard for all Aston Martins to follow. A year later, DB2s finished in first, second and third places in the 3.0-litre class at Le Mans.

In 1954, David Brown bought another company – a decision that was going to be a significant part of Aston Martin's history – he took over the ailing Tickford Motor Bodies which was based in Newport Pagnell. Tickford

▲ The DB5 that was used in the James Bond film Goldfinger

was a long-established company that had begun by building horse-drawn carriages and went on to, by coincidence, build bodies for Lagonda.

Up until Brown taking over Tickford, Aston Martin production had been somewhat dispersed, with bodies built by Mulliner in Birmingham, engines and gearboxes by Brown's Huddersfield factory, and assembly taking place at the Feltham workshops. Now, though, production could be centralised

at Newport Pagnell.

During this period, Aston Martin development continued, with the road cars now very separate to the racers. This led to some confusing names. For instance, the DB3 of 1951 was a racing car designed by Dr Robert Eberan von Ebervorst, a German who had worked for EWA before moving to Aston Martin. The car he created was an open two-seater with a 2.6-litre engine that proved a disappointment in competition.

In 1953 came the DB2/4; essentially a two-plus-two version of the DB2 with two small rear seats and a larger boot. This was followed two years later by the DB2/4 Mark II, which was little more than a mid-life facelift of the same car.

Then, in 1957 came the DB2's replacement. No, not the DB3 because that name had already been taken by the aforementioned racecar, but the DB Mark III. Not surprisingly this did, and still does, cause confusion, with many people incorrectly referring to the road car as a 'DB3'. Even Ian Fleming got it wrong in Goldfinger, the first James Bond novel to mention an Aston Martin.

Thankfully, by the time the next model came along, Aston Martin had got its numbering back on track and the new car of 1958 was called the DB4. However, that went on to have four updates, with the original becoming known as the DB4 Series 1, going up to the Series 5 of 1962.

During this period, Aston Martin as a company continued to lose money, which caused David Brown a lot of trouble. Motorsport had continued to take up a large part of the company's resources and, despite successes such as winning the World Sportscar Championship in 1959, Brown took the decision to withdraw all factory motorsport involvement at the end of the 1963 season. In the same year, the DB5 was launched, a car that was an obvious evolution of the DB4, rather than a new model in its own right.

However, by 1965 a new model did appear. That was the DB6, which was a much-improved car in all ways. Unfortunately, though, it didn't sell that well during the five years of its life; partly because it was considered old-fashioned by some buyers. As ever, then, Aston Martin continued to struggle financially.

The company fought back against the accusations that the DB6 was dated with a brand-new model – the DBS of 1967.

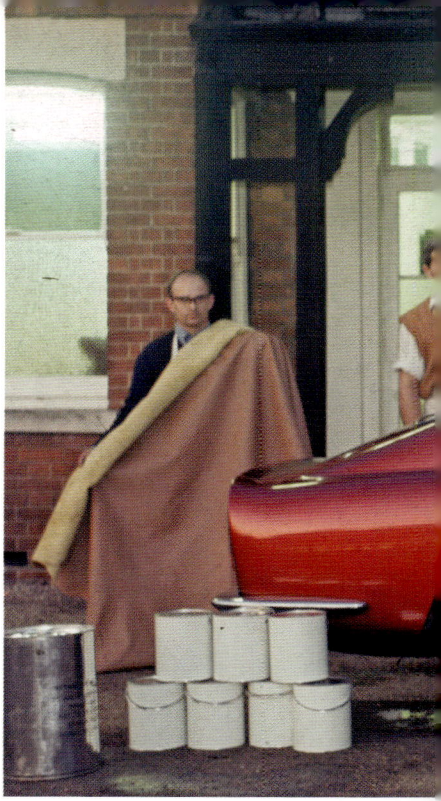

Penned by Aston Martin's ambitious new designer, William Towns, it was a wider, more angular and more aggressive car. It was a style that set the tone of Aston Martins for the next 25 years.

William Towns had begun his career working for Rootes, where he designed

the Hillman Hunter. He then moved to Rover and then to Aston Martin, where he started off designing seats before his talent was spotted. He stayed with Aston Martin until 1977.

Originally, it was planned to fit the DBS with a new V8 engine developed by Tadek Marek but, in the event, the 4.0-litre DB6 unit was used instead. However, a V8 version did follow in 1970. There was also a four-door saloon version which was badged as a Lagonda, but only a handful were built.

▲ The DB5 is unveiled in 1967

New owners

BY THE START OF THE 1970S, the David Brown Group was struggling. Tractor sales were down and, by 1972, Aston Martin Lagonda was some half a million pounds in debt. Brown had had enough and sold the car company for just £100 to a consortium of Midlands-based businessmen called Company Developments. Brown, though, remained onboard as president. The new chairman, William Wilson, reduced costs wherever he could and dropped the 'DB' model designations. Instead, the updated DBS-derived cars were called Aston Martin Vantage (in six-cylinder form) and Aston Martin V8. These were heavily – and expensively – updated to enable them to be sold in the US market.

Once again, though, the company ended up in financial trouble and, shockingly, asked the UK government for help in 1974 before finally going into liquidation. The following year, Aston Martin was again bought out, this time by two North American businessmen George Minden and Peter Sprague. Minden was a Canadian Rolls Royce

◀ The personal Lagonda of David Brown. The car is a lengthened four-door version of the 170mph Aston Martin DBS-V8

dealer and was passionate about Aston Martins. Sprague, meanwhile, hailed from the USA and was also a fan of the marque, as well as a successful businessman who specialised in taking over ailing companies. They were soon joined by Englishmen, Alan Curtis and Denis Flather, again both Aston

PUR 101R

Martin enthusiasts.

The plan was to modernise the model line-up and restore the public's faith in this once proud marque. What was needed was an exciting new car that would attract attention, so William Towns was called upon to come up with something.

The result was the astonishingly futuristic Aston Martin Lagonda, which was first shown to the public in 1976, but it wouldn't go into production for another two years. With its sharp lines and electronic dashboard, the exciting Lagonda certainly got the world's attention and convinced people that Aston Martin once again had a future. No matter that, under the skin, the Lagonda was little more than a rebodied Aston Martin V8.

By now, the six-cylinder model line had been dropped, and the Aston Martin range consisted of the V8 Vantage and V8 Volante – the latter being an open-top version. Both cars were very obviously evolutions of Towns' DBS.

Towns also designed another car for Aston Martin but it remained a one-off concept. It was the Bulldog, a stunning two-seater sportscar with a mid-mounted, 650bhp V8 engine and gullwing doors. It was very low at just one-metre high and had an array of five headlamps hidden behind the low bonnet panel, which dropped down to reveal the lights at night.

The Bulldog reached a top speed of 191mph during testing, although Aston Martin claimed a speed in excess of 200mph was possible. The prototype was sold to a private buyer after the 1980 launch and no more were built which is, perhaps, a good thing. While the Bulldog was undoubtedly stunning, it had very little about it that said 'Aston Martin' – it could have had any badge on it.

A rather less exotic prototype from the pen of William Towns also appeared in 1980. At this time, the Abingdon-based MG marque was in trouble and Aston Martin had plans to buy it, thus sensibly giving them a budget sportscar brand to sit alongside the prestigious Aston Martin and Lagonda names. The plan came to nothing, though, but not before Towns had designed a moderately facelifted MGB Roadster with plastic side panels and a lower roof line.

◀ The 1976 Aston Martin – the Lagonda

Victor Gauntlett

THE SAME YEAR SAW ASTON MARTIN change hands once again. By this time, the current incumbents had had enough and only Peter Sprague and Alan Curtis were left at the helm. There were, though, two new investors, Tim Hearley and Victor Gauntlett.

Hearley ran CH Industrials which produced car parts, while Victor Gauntlett was an English entrepreneur who owned Pace Petroleum. At the beginning of 1981, the two men took over control of Aston Martin Lagonda, with Gauntlett as chairman, while still running Pace at the same time. Gauntlett swiftly reintroduced a motorsport programme, cleverly using Pace as a sponsor.

Just two years after this latest upheaval, Pace sold its share of the business to an American Aston Martin dealership, Automotive Investments, on

the condition that Gauntlett continued as chairman of Aston Martin. To free up his time Gauntlett then sold Pace Petroleum to the Kuwait Investment Trust.

Soon after, CH Industrials also sold out to Automotive Investments, thus giving the latter a 100 percent stake in Aston Martin. This arrangement, though, was short-lived because Automotive Investments had other financial commitments. Therefore, Gauntlett engineered a deal whereby he took over 25 percent of the company, while Peter Livano, a Greek shipping magnate, bought the balance.

Now he had more funding, the charismatic Victor Gauntlett set about turning around Aston Martin with gusto. Although he knew that the company's long-term survival depended on selling greater volumes, that wasn't possible without massive investment, so he concentrated on the top end of the market, with the expensive V8 Zagato, which launched in 1986. This was the spiritual successor to the DB4 Zagato in that it was a two-seater based on the V8, but with a shortened chassis.

It was designed by the Italian Zagato company and was strikingly modern in appearance. Looks were deceptive, though, because underneath it was all good old-fashioned muscle car, with its V8 engine developing 438bhp – enough to propel the relatively lightweight supercar to 186mph. Compared to the contemporary high-tech Porsche 959 the Zagato was crude – it didn't even have ABS – but no matter, the market for rare cars was buoyant and Aston Martin had an eager queue of potential buyers for its latest creation. An open-top Volante version following a year later.

▲ The V8 Zagato proved to be a useful money-maker for Aston Martin

The Ford connection

IN 1987, VICTOR GAUNTLETT found himself at the Mille Miglia retrospective, chatting to Walter Hayes, vice-president of Ford Europe, who had an interest in classic marques. Gauntlett explained his vision for a higher volume Aston Martin and Hayes pricked up his ears. Events moved quickly and, by September of that year Ford had bought a 75 percent stake in Aston Martin, with an agreement that Gauntlett would remain in charge for at least two years.

With Ford's backing it was now possible to retire the by now 20-year-old V8 cars, which were really starting to show their age. In its place came the Virage of 1990, which was designed by John Heffernan and Ken Greeley. Sensibly, the Virage's lines were an evolution of what came before it, rather than a radical reinterpretation of the marque. It retained the muscular stance of

▶The Virage was very fresh and modern looking

the V8 but in a smoother, more integrated way, and there was even a hint of BD4 in it.

To ensure worldwide compliance and the use of unleaded petrol, the trusty V8 engine was shipped off to Reeves Calloway Engineering in the USA for a thorough overhaul. The new engine had four valves per cylinder and catalytic converters, and produced a respectable 310bhp in its initial form.

The Virage was, though, still an expensive motorcar, lovingly hand-built at Aston Martin's Newport Pagnell headquarters. Hardly what you'd expect of a company backed by Ford. Victor Gauntlett was still arguing for a less expensive, larger volume modern car that would generate some real income and, not surprisingly, Ford was in total agreement.

▲ The DB7 was one of the most successful Aston Martin's of all time

The parent company had the engineering and other resources necessary to make this happen. Gauntlett, by this time, had decided he had done all he could and so handed the reins over to Walter Hayes in 1991.

Hayes was a good man for the job. After working as a journalist, he had

been instrumental in the development of, among other things, the Lotus Cortina and the Ford GT40 racing car before running Ford's worldwide PR department in the early 1980s.

By 1993, Ford had bought the remaining 25 percent of the company, so it now had a 100 percent stake, which it placed under the Premier Automotive Group (which also controlled Jaguar). This meant that Walter Hayes was finally able to make his predecessor's dream of a larger-volume Aston Martin a reality. The Jaguar connection meant that Hayes was able to share some of the development costs and parts with that of the new XK8. It also gave him a new factory – the Bloxham facility in Oxfordshire that had been used for the XJ220 supercar – in which to build the new Aston Martin.

The brief was to create something in the spirit of the old DB4, so a Jaguar-based, 3.2-litre six-cylinder supercharged engine was sourced, along with a chassis from the Jaguar XJS. The bodywork of the new car was designed by Ian Callum, chief designer at TWR Design, and was a reinterpretation of the DB4 to DB6 range, rather than a follow-on from the later – and

▲ The DB7's interior was a sumptuous blend of traditional and modern

larger – V8 cars. The result was achingly beautiful and thoroughly modern, rather than a pastiche of the earlier cars; even though the DB4 heritage was obvious.

Walter Hayes invited Sir David Brown – as he was by now – to take a look at the prototype of the new car, and the 89-year-old was thrilled by it. It was agreed that the car be called the DB7 and Brown admitted that this name was almost used for the DB6 Mark II and he even had some old badges to prove it. Brown was made lifetime president of Aston Martin in recognition of what he had done for the marque – a nice touch

and a great bit of marketing, too. Sadly, though, Brown died soon after, so he never saw the new car go on sale.

The DB7 was very well received, with the exception of some critics who compared it to the Jaguar XK8 (which was much cheaper) and complained about the presence of Ford switchgear inside – one wag responded to this by pointing out that an Aston Martin buyer wouldn't know what the inside of a Ford looked like!

Despite the idea of producing a volume car, the DB7 was anything but, by Ford's standards. That said, it broke Aston Martin records when, in 1995, 700 cars were built. By 1998, a total of 2000 DB7s had been built and, four years later, 6000 – far more than the combined total production of the DB5 and DB6. By comparison, back in 1993, when the UK was in recession, just 46 Aston Martins had been built all year, so this was all good news for the marque.

The DB7 opened up a whole new market of buyers to Aston Martin – people who wanted a more accessible car that was easy to live with on a day-to-day basis – and that was increased further by the launch of the open-top Volante in 1997, which was especially popular with female buyers.

The model was extended in 1999 with the V12-powered DB7 Vantage that gave the car the performance to match its looks and went on to be a great success. So much so, in fact, that the six-cylinder version was discontinued soon after.

At the same time all this was going on, the company hadn't forgotten its heritage and, over at Newport Pagnell, they were still making hand-built cars for the hard-core enthusiasts and super-rich. These were based on the Virage design but renamed Vantage. Big and muscular, the Vantage combined a lightweight aluminium bodyshell with a powerful supercharged V8 engine that produced 550bhp.

By this time, though, car building at Newport Pagnell was very limited and a large part of the historic facility was, therefore, put to good use servicing and restoring customer's own cars – from early classics to the current range, thus ensuring that customers received the best possible care for their beloved Aston Martins.

Dr Ulich Bez

▶ The DB7 Vantage with its beautiful and timeless lines

▼ Ulrich Bez, a keen racing driver, was appointed Chairman of Aston Martin in 2000

IN JULY 2000, ASTON MARTIN GOT a new boss when Dr Ulich Bez became chairman and chief executive. German-born Bez had a Doctorate in Engineering from the University of Berlin and had previously been responsible for product design and development at Porsche, BMW and Daewoo. Previous to his joining Aston Martin he was a business adviser to the Ford Motor Company in the USA.

A year after Bez's appointment, in 2001, a brand-new model appeared out of Newport Pagnell. Designed by Ian Callum, Bez insisted that this flagship supercar should be stripped of any recognisable Ford parts (it was to have had Ka air vents, for instance) before it went into production. The Vanquish was a mix of DB7 styling with Vantage size and aggression, and used high-tech materials, such as carbon fibre and aluminium in its lightweight construction. Under that long bonnet was a 6.0-litre V12 engine that produced 469bhp and was linked to a six-speed automatic transmission with Formula One-style paddle shifters.

Then, in 2002, Aston Martin renewed its links with Zagato, the Italian styling company, to produce a spiritual successor to the DB4 Zagato of 1961 and the V8 Vantage Zagato of 1986. The result was the limited edition DB7 Zagato, of which just 99 were built. Based on the V12 DB7 Vantage, this car had a restyled aluminium bodyshell with a massive, bulbous front grille and a distinctive 'double bubble' roofline. It was, perhaps, less good-looking than the standard DB7 but that didn't stop the cars being snapped up by eager buyers, no doubt hopeful that they would prove to be a good long-term investment. An open-top version, named DB American Roadster 1, followed and, again, just 99 examples were built.

There was no doubt that Aston Martin was on a roll at this time –

DB7 VANTAGE

▲ The AMV8 Vantage at the Geneva International Motor Show in 2003

a fact that was confirmed when, in 2003, it unveiled the AMV8 Vantage concept car at the Detroit Motor Show. Here was a lithe and lean sportscar that could compete with the likes of the Porsche 911, in terms of price, performance and usability. It also looked stunning and the world was eager to see it go into production.

That, though, was just a glimpse into the future; in the meantime, Aston Martin was readying a replacement for the DB7. Although, with the aforementioned V8 Vantage in the wings, this

▲ Devotees of the Aston Martin marque admiring the DB9 at the Frankfurt Motor Show in 2003

new car was to be more upmarket and only available with a V12 engine. The DB8 badge was skipped over, because it was thought it would cause confusion with the entry-level V8, and so the DB9 name was used instead.

The DB7 went out with a bang, with the limited edition DB7 GT, and the DB9 was launched at the Frankfurt Motor Show on 9 September 2003. The Henrik Fisker styling was more aggressive than that of the DB7 – more in keeping with the Vanquish, in fact. At the same time, though, it was an astonishingly 'clean' design, refreshingly free of shutlines, rain channels and other clutter.

▶ The beautifully hand crafted V12 Vanquish S

New home at Gaydon

WITH THE VANQUISH STILL BEING built in small numbers at Newport Pagnell and the prospect of making large amounts of both the DB9 and V8 Vantage, it was clear that the small factory at Bloxham was not going to be adequate. Happily, though, Ford had recently taken over Land Rover and the deal included a development site in nearby Gaydon, in Warwickshire.

It was at Gaydon that the first-ever purpose-built Aston Martin plant was built. Behind the stunning curved sandstone façade – which was claimed to emulate an English country estate, while at the same time remaining ultra-modern – lay a state-of-the-art facility that dragged Aston Martin firmly into the 21st century. "Gaydon is the future of Aston Martin. It combines cutting-edge technology with hand-craftsmanship and tradition. It is probably the best facility

of its type in the world, and the perfect showcase of how to design and build innovative sports and GT cars for the 21st century," claimed a proud Dr Ulrich Bez.

The company was also keen to stress that, despite the new factory embracing new technology, the cars were certainly not mass-produced, with each DB9 taking no less than 200 man-hours to create. Indeed, there was only one robot in the factory, in the body-in-white area, to aid with the high-tech bonding

▼ The graceful but powerful Rapide Concept

processes for the aluminium panels. Even the paint was sprayed by hand, with this process alone taking up to 25 hours to perfect.

The excitement continued in December 2003, when Aston Martin announced that it would return to motor racing in 2005. A new division, called Aston Martin Racing, was formed which worked with nearby Prodrive to develop the DBR9 racecar for competing in the GT class of sportscar races, including the

prestigious Le Mans 24-Hour.

In 2004, Aston Martin unveiled the open-top – and very beautiful – DB9 Volante at the Detroit Motor Show. Meanwhile, over at Newport Pagnell, they'd been far from lazy, as was proved by the Vanquish S which was launched at the 2004 Paris Motor Show. This was the fastest production model ever built by Aston Martin, with a maximum speed of over 200mph thanks to a 6.0-litre V12 engine that developed a healthy 520mph.

That was an impressive machine, for sure, but of far more relevance from a commercial point of view was the launch of the production version of the V8 Vantage on 1 March 2005 at the Geneva Motor Show. This remained essentially similar to the AM V8 concept car and offered a combination of good looks with practicality for two people. The mid-front-mounted V8 engine ensured excellent road-holding and, with 380bhp on tap, superb performance, too. The car was aimed directly at the Porsche 911 Turbo market, in terms of price, performance, size and handling. The Vantage did, however, offer an air of quality and exclusivity that had become somewhat

◀ The elegant V8 Vantage with its perfect proportions

▲ The V8 Vantage debuting at the 75th Geneva Motor Show in 2005

▶ The Vantage is powered by a 4.3 quad cam 32 valve V8 engine

lost from the German classic. An open-top version of the Vantage followed in 2006 and was badged Roadster. Aston Martin also produced a race-prepared version called the Nürburgring 24hr V8 Vantage – or simply N24.

Also in 2006 came the news that the 30,000 Aston Martins had been built, plus exciting plans for future models.

First off, at the Detroit Motor Show, appeared the Rapide four-door concept car. Essentially a stretched DB9, the Rapide was the spiritual successor to Lagonda of the 1970s and proved that a saloon car could combine style and performance with practicality. "In terms of elegance the Rapide is adding value to the DB9's undisputed elegance and subtle understatement," enthused Dr Ulrich Bez. "The proportions must be perfect. If we couldn't achieve this then we wouldn't have made the car," he continued.

What made the Rapide feasible was what Aston Martin called its VH (Vertical/Horizontal) architecture. This high-strength, low-mass system formed the backbone of the DB9. The extruded aluminium construction could be modified in both length and width, provide the chemically-bonded structure (using glues derived from aircraft manufacture) was mated with the aluminium and composite bodywork.

The other exciting new car of 2006 was the DBS which made its debut in grand fashion as James Bond's car in the film, Casino Royale. Although Aston Martin didn't reveal too much about the car, it was very obviously a link between the road-going DB9 and the race-prepared DBR9, with more power, a stripped-out interior and enhanced aerodynamics. "The DBS does not have the understated elegance of a DB9, nor the youthful agility of the V8 Vantage. It is explosive power in a black tie and

▲ The Rapide on display at the 2006 Geneva Motor Show

has its own unique character which will equal that of James Bond," explained an enthusiastic Dr Ulrich Bez.

It was all looking very promising. At long last, Aston Martin had the funds and facilities to produce a range of superb cars that would actually make the company money. Unfortunately, though, by 2006, parent company Ford was not making money and felt it was time to sell off parts of its Premium Automotive Group, of which Aston Martin was a part. It was decided that the other UK brands, Jaguar Cars and Land Rover, plus Volvo Cars, had more potential (being larger volume) than the relatively niche-market, but profit-making, Aston Martin. In August 2006, Ford announced that it may be willing to sell all or part of Aston Martin. "As part of our on-going strategic review, we have determined that Aston Martin may be an attractive opportunity to raise capital and generate value," explained William Clay Ford Jr, Ford's executive chairman.

▲ David Richards, the non-executive chairman of Aston Martin

The future

ON 12TH MARCH IT WAS announced that Aston Martin had been purchased by a consortium for £475-million. However, Ford retained a £40-million stake in the company. The consortium was led by Prodrive Chairman, David Richards, and also consisted of John Sinders, an Aston Martin collector, and two Kuwaiti investment companies.

So, it's hard to know what the future holds for Aston Martin. As we have seen, the company has a long history of uncertainty, with jumps from one owner to the next. There's no doubt, though, that Ford has done wonders in turning Aston Martin round and putting it on a secure footing for the future. The cars and production facilities are second to none, and the DB9 platform has the flexibility to be developed into new models.

It is possible that Aston Martin will be better placed free from the huge Ford corporate culture. However, these days it's hard for small car companies to exist without the backing of a larger corporation. Whatever happens, though, you can be sure that the marque (the word brand surely doesn't appeal) will continue to excite and surprise us for many years to come as it heads speedily towards its second century.

Aston Martin Timeline

1914
Aston Martin name is born, following success at the Aston Clinton Hillclimb.

1915
First Aston Martin is registered.

1921
First works competition car makes its appearance.

1922
Aston Martin makes first appearance overseas at French Grand Prix.

1924
Charnwood family lend financial support.

1925
Company forced to close.

1926
Aston Martin Motors Limited is formed and sets up in Feltham.

1928
Aston Martin's first entry at the Le Mans 24-Hour race.

1932
Sutherland family takes over the company.

1937
140 cars built – the highest pre-war production figure.

1939
The Atom is built. **1946**
Aston Martin is advertised for sale in The Times.

1947
David Brown buys Aston Martin Motors Limited and Lagonda.

1948
The Spa Special wins the Spa 24-Hour race. Aston Martin 2-litre is built.

1950
DB2 goes into production.

1951
DB2s come first, second and third in the 3.0-litre class at Le Mans.

1953
DB2/4 goes into production – the first two-plus-two Aston Martin.

1954
David Brown buys Tickfords and moves production to Newport Pagnell.

1955
DB2/4 Mark II goes into production.

1956
During this and the following three years, four DBR1 race cars are built for competition.

1957
DB Mk III goes into production.

1958
DB4 goes into production.

1959
Aston Martin wins World Sportscar Championship in the DBR1 following wins at the 1000kms at the Nürburgring, Le Mans and the RAC Tourist Trophy.

1963
Roy Salvadori wins at Monza in a DB4GT. DB5 goes into production.

1965
DB6 goes into production.

1967
DBS goes into production.

1969
DB6 Mark II and DBSV8 go into production.

1972
David Brown forced to sell and Company Developments takes over. Aston Martin Vantage and Aston Martin V8 go into production.

1975
Receivership declared and company rescued by consortium led by Peter Sprague and George Minden. Production hits an all-time low of 21.

1976
William Towns-designed Aston Martin Lagonda saloon unveiled.

1977
V8 Vantage goes into production.

1978
V8 Volante goes into production.

1980
Towns' Lagonda goes into production.

1981
Victor Gauntlett and Pace Petroleum take over.

1983
Victor Gauntlett is backed financially by the Livanos shipping family.

1986
V8 Vantage Zagato goes into production.

1987
V8 Volante Zagato goes into production.

1987
Ford Motor Company takes a 75 percent shareholding.

1989
Works supported AMR1 comes sixth in the World Championship.

1990
Virage production starts.

1991
Victor Gauntlett resigns and is replaced by Walter Hayes.

1992
Virage Volante goes into production.

1993
Vantage goes into production.

1994
Ford Motor Company acquires 100 percent holding in Aston Martin. DB7 goes into production.

1996
DB7 Volante and V8 Coupe go into production.

1997
V8 Volante goes into production.

1999
V8 Vantage Le Mans and DB7 Vantage go into production.

2001
The 5000th DB7 is built.

2001
V12 Vanquish goes into production.

2002
After almost 15 years, Aston Martin renews its relationship with Italian coachbuilders Zagato to produce the limited edition DB7 Zagato.

2003
Aston Martin unveils the AMV8 Vantage concept car at the Detroit Motor Show.

2003
DB9 goes into production.

2003
The new Gaydon manufacturing facility is officially opened. It is the first purpose-built factory in Aston Martin's history.

2004
DB9 Volante is revealed at the Detroit Motor Show.

2004
Aston Martin announces its intention to return to sportscar racing with DBR9.

2005
V8 Vantage is launched at the Geneva Motor Show.

2005
DB9 Volante goes into production.

2006
Aston Martin unveils the Rapide four-door concept car at the Detroit Motor Show.

2006
The 30,000th Aston Martin rolls off the production line at Gaydon.

2006
Aston Martin announces the production version of the V8 Vantage N24.

2006
New Aston Martin DBS seen for the first time in the James Bond film Casino Royale.

2006
Aston Martin unveils the V8 Vantage Roadster at the LA Motor Show.

2007
Aston Martin sold to consortium of investors, with Ford retaining a stake.

Chapter 2

David Brown

ALTHOUGH MANY PEOPLE HAVE been instrumental in the development and success of Aston Martin over the years, one man in particular deserves a closer look, if only because his initials have become synonymous with the marque.

David Brown was born on 10 May 1904 in Huddersfield, Yorkshire, the son of Frank Brown who, with his brother Percy, was the owner of David Brown & Sons Limited, which had been formed by David's grandfather, David Brown senior, in 1898 and specialised in making machine-cut gearwheels.

At the age of 17, the young David Brown started work as an apprentice in the family business, which by then was manufacturing self-contained worm gear units (by 1921 it was the largest worm gear manufacturer in the world). It seems that he was given no special treatment as the son of the boss, as he had to walk a mile-and-a-half to the railway station each morning, followed by a similar distance to the factory – and he was expected to start work at 7am each morning! After a similar journey home each day, the tireless teenager then went to evening classes twice a week to ensure a rounded education. Later, though, his father gave him a motorcycle for the journey to work. In typical fashion, the youngster pulled the machine to pieces and rebuilt it with a modified engine and went on to use it successfully in hillclimb events.

Indeed, Brown could well have been

▲ The DB 2D built in 1958

a professional racing driver if his father had not suffered a stroke, meaning that he was needed in the family business. At the age of 25, David Brown became a director of the company and, when his Uncle Percy died in 1931, he became managing director, with his father, Frank, as chairman.

In 1934, the company moved to new premises at Meltham to the south of

Huddersfield. It was here that, in 1939, they started to build tractors, in conjunction with Ferguson. During the Second World War, the factory was kept busy making gears for aircraft use and also tank transmissions (they produced over 10,000 of the latter).

Also during the war, the company launched the heavy duty David Brown tractor, of which more than 7700 were sold, making good profits. The name David Brown became well-known among farming circles.

Brown enjoyed his wealth; he owned race-horses and played polo as well as racing cars and motorcycles. What's more, he liked to fly aeroplanes and pilot speedboats. One of his many boats boasted two 2000bhp engines and reached speeds of 45mph.

With this background, it was perhaps no surprise that he was intrigued by the classified advertisement in The Times late in 1946. The tiny announcement read:

High-Class Motor Business, established 25 years: £30,000: net profits last year £4,000. – Write Box V.1362, The Times, E.C.4.

As we've seen, Brown ended up buying Aston Martin for £20,500 – substantially less than the asking price, but still a significant amount of money – and it was his own personal money, not from his company.

Owning Aston Martin allowed Brown to indulge his passion for motorsport and, although he never competed at Le Mans, he made it his business to drive one of the bruised and battered racecars back to the UK and, by all accounts, enjoyed every minute of the arduous journey. However, in his private life he often drove a Jaguar, not an Aston Martin.

During the 1950s, the David Brown Group expanded to produce gears for car transmission and, not surprisingly, these were used in Aston Martins.

Brown was knighted in 1968 and then sold Aston Martin in 1972. In the same year, he sold the ailing tractor division of his company to a US concern, which renamed it Case.

He retained ownership of the David Brown Group until that was sold in 1990. Three years later, it was floated on the London Stock Exchange and, in 1998, the David Brown Group was taken over by Textron Inc and is still a major producer of heavy duty gear products.

Brown married three times, to Daisy Muriel Firth in 1926, Marjorie Deans (his secretary) in 1955, and to Paula Benton Stone in 1980. He had two children, David and Angela, both of whom entered the family business. Angela married George Abecassis, the racing driver.

On his retirement, the wealthy David Brown moved to Monaco to avoid paying high rates of UK tax, but kept a farm in Buckinghamshire where he enjoyed keeping cattle.

Brown died, aged 89, on 3 September 1993, just before the Aston Martin DB7 – the first new Aston Martin to bear his initials since the DBS of 1967 – went into production. However, his name – and especially his famous initials will always live on as an integral part of the Aston Martin brand.

◀ Sir David Brown who executed a takeover of Aston Martin in 1947

Aston Martin through the ages

International
1929-1932

WHEN CESARE BERTELLI BECAME involved with Aston Martin, he wanted the company's cars to be reliable enough to take you from England to France, compete in the Le Mans 24-Hour race and then drive the car home again, all in comfort.

The road-going solution that he came up with was the International, so named because it was designed to comply with the regulations of the international motorsport governing body, AIACR (Association Internationale des Automobile Clubs Reconnus).

The car was powered by a 1.5-litre engine that had been designed by Claude Hill, who would go on to be responsible for the radical Atom. It was a simple, overhead camshaft unit that offered the required reliability and had dry-sump lubrication so it could be mounted low in the body. To optimise the car's handling, the chassis was under-slung to ensure a low centre of gravity, and to give the car a low and sporty appearance.

The majority of Internationals were two-seater, open-top cars, although a long-chassis version was offered which had room in the back for two passengers. There was also a very pretty fixed-head coupe that was built to special order – one of the advantages of a separate chassis was that it was relatively simple to fit custom-made bodywork.

In 1931, Aston Martin offered a more race-inspired version of the car, which was the International Le Mans (not to be confused with the later car that was called simply 'Le Mans'). This was mechanically similar to the standard car but had sleeker bodywork that was based on the company's team racecars of the period.

The following year, the International was heavily revised in an attempt to make it less expensive to produce. This was retrospectively known as the 'New International' and only about a dozen are believed to have been built. It had a new chassis design and a cheaper transmission system, and could be identified by its tapered radiator. Incidentally, the 'New International' was the first Aston Martin to feature the now famous winged badge, although it was dropped from the subsequent Le Mans model.

SPECIFICATION

Engine: Four inline cylinders with overhead camshaft

Capacity: 1494cc

Bore x stroke: 69x99mm

Maximum Power: 56bhp at 4250rpm

Maximum Torque: n/a

Transmission: Four-speed manual

Suspension: Front: Rigid axle with leaf springs. Rear: Live axle with leaf springs.

Length: 3900mm

Width: 1640mm

Height: 1300mm

Weight: 860kg

Top Speed: 75mph

0-60mph: n/a

Le Mans
1932-1933

ASTON MARTIN WAS STRUGGLING to make any money at the start of the 1930s, partly because of the poor economic climate and partly because its cars were expensive to produce and the company was going through a difficult time, with various investors coming and going.

The so-called New International of 1931 addressed the cost issue to some extent but was not a sales success, so a new model was developed with which

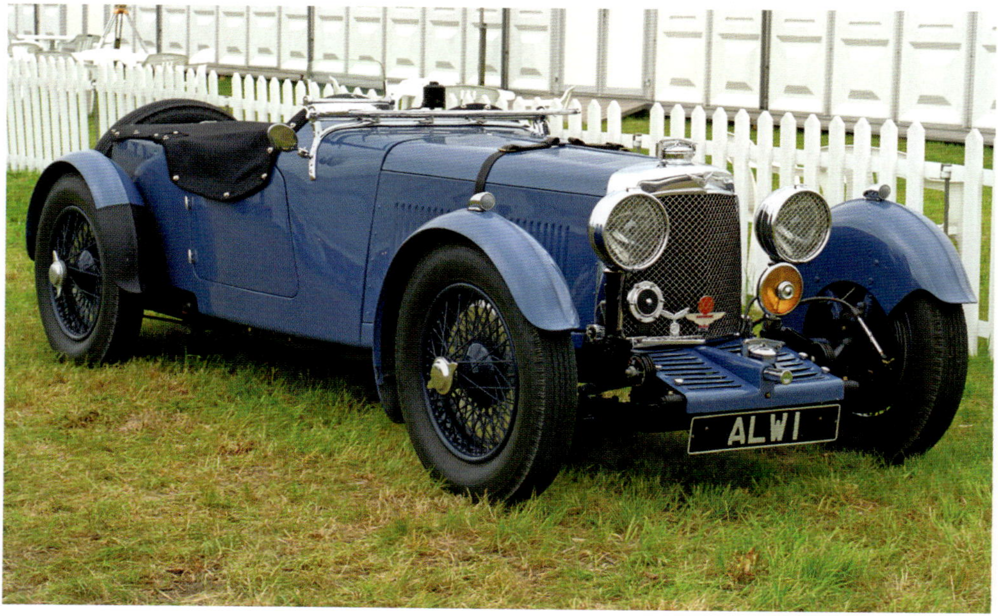

to tempt customers.

That new car was known as the Le Mans (not to be confused with the earlier International Le Mans) in deference to the company's ongoing success at the famous French endurance race.

Although mechanically similar, and with a same basic chassis, the Le Mans had restyled bodywork with a lower, squatter radiator that was designed to make the car push through the air more efficiently. The aerodynamics were also improved by a hood that folded flush with the bodywork – in those days, people drove with the roof down in all but the most inclement weather, even when racing – and, as before, the front cycle wings moved as the steering turned. The Le Mans was offered in two- and four-seater form; the latter with a longer chassis.

The engine of the Le Mans was essentially the same Claude Hill four-cylinder, 1.5-litre unit as used in the previous International. However, for the new car, it had been uprated with magnesium pistons, a higher compression ratio, twin electric fuel pumps (the driver could control which one was operating) and other refinements that upped the power to an extravagant (for its day) 70bhp, which was enough to drive the lightweight car at speeds of over 80mph.

Despite the best attempts of the company's engineers, the Le Mans ended up costing some £120 more than the equivalent International, at £595 in two-seater form. Bizarrely, though, it turned out to be a much more successful car for Aston Martin, with more than 100 examples being sold in 1932 and 1933. Just 15 of these were the long-wheelbase, four-seater cars.

SPECIFICATION

Engine: Four inline cylinders with overhead camshaft
Capacity: 1494cc
Bore x stroke: 69x99mm
Maximum Power: 70bhp at 4750rpm
Maximum Torque: n/a
Transmission: Four-speed manual
Suspension: Front: Rigid axle with leaf springs. Rear: Live axle with leaf springs
Length: 4050mm
Width: 1680mm
Height: 1230mm
Weight: 1020kg
Top Speed: 84mph
0-60mph: n/a

Mark II and Ulster

1934-1935

BY THE EARLY 1930S, ASTON MARTIN was owned by the Sutherland family and they were keen to make the company profitable. One solution they came up with was to broaden the marque's appeal by moving away from race-orientated cars, such as the Le Mans, and towards something rather more refined and sophisticated. Looking back, this was a decision that was going to have a long-term influence on future Aston Martins as this was the direction most models would take.

The first car to adopt this policy was the Mark II of 1934. This used essentially the same chassis as the Le Mans, albeit stiffened and fitted with a different front suspension to improve the road-holding somewhat.

The car was available in short and long wheelbase form, the latter with a reasonable amount of space for rear passengers. The short wheelbase version was available only as an open-top car,

while the long wheelbase could also be had in tourer and saloon body styles. The Mark II retained the squat radiator of the Le Mans but this time it was visually enhanced with smart vertical slats instead of mesh. This not only gave the car a classy appearance, the slats also opened and closed via a thermostat to control the air flow. As was by now an Aston Martin trademark, the front cycle wings moved with the steering.

The Mark II was powered by the same four-cylinder, 1.5-litre engine as used in the Le Mans, albeit slightly tweaked to produce 73bhp, and the power was fed to the rear wheels via a four-speed gearbox.

A racing car was developed from the Mark II and these proved very successful in competition, winning first, second and third in class at the 1934 Ulster Tourist Trophy. This led to a replica version, called the Ulster, being made for the public to buy.

The Ulster, of which just 21 were built, had a similar body to the race cars; low and narrow with a sleek boat-shaped tail that contained the spare wheel. Because previous Aston Martin racing cars had been painted British Racing Green and had been unlucky in competition, Cesare Bertelli, who was looking after the racing side of the business, decided to opt for bright red – the colour of his home country, Italy.

Crucially, the Ulster was guaranteed to reach the magical 100mph mark. This was made possible by way of a tuned version of the Mark II engine. A higher compression ratio (9.5:1), along with polished ports and larger SU carburettors, combined to push the maximum power output to 85bhp.

SPECIFICATION

Engine: Four inline cylinders with overhead camshaft
Capacity: 1494cc
Bore x stroke: 69x99mm
Maximum Power: 73bhp at 4750rpm
Maximum Torque: n/a
Transmission: Four-speed manual
Suspension: Front: Rigid axle with leaf springs. Rear: Live axle with leaf springs
Length: 3850mm
Width: 1630mm
Height: 1200mm
Weight: 870kg
Top Speed: 92mph
0-60mph: n/a

15/98

1936-1939

WITH THE 15/98 OF 1936, ASTON Martin moved even further from its sporting roots in an attempt to increase market share. The name referred to the engine's RAC taxable horsepower (15) and actual horsepower (98bhp). Respectable figures that were used in cars that were more high-speed tourers

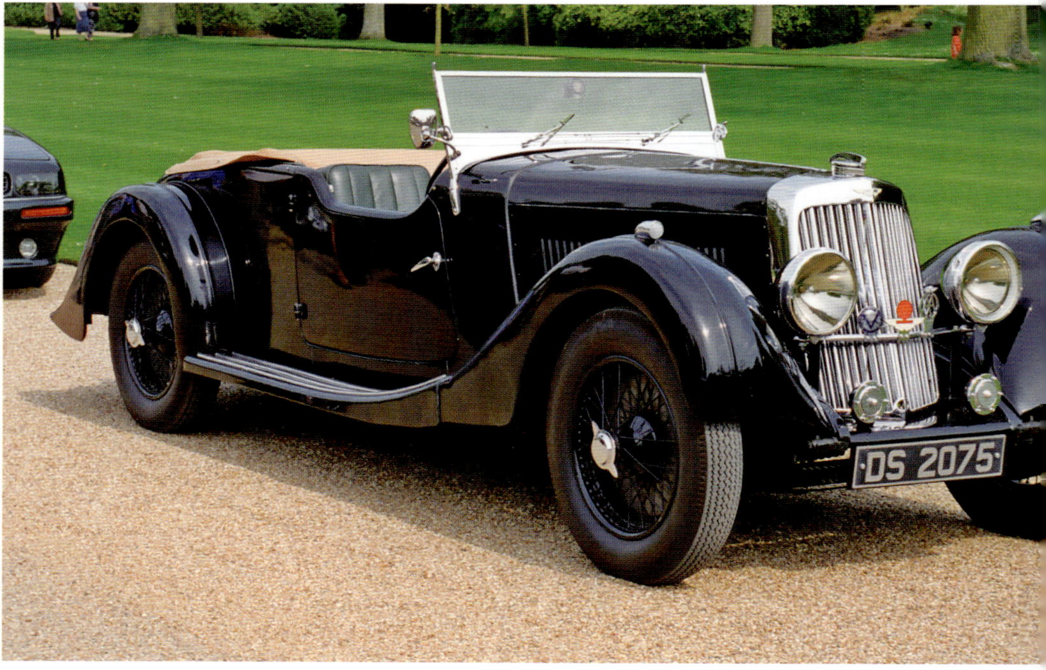

than out and out sports cars.

The 15/98 was powered by a 2.0-litre four-cylinder engine that had been developed from the previous 1.5-litre unit, with the inlet and exhaust ports reversed to improve efficiency.

Styling-wise, the 15/98 was a very different car, indeed. Offered in short and long chassis versions, buyers could choose from open-top tourers, drophead coupes or a closed saloon. Gone were the previous cycle wings, to be replaced with more modern fixed front wings that swept back to meet the running boards, as was the fashion of the day. The rear wings aped the fronts and swept back into a streamlined rear panel.

It was undoubtedly an elegant car and one designed for touring rather than racing. Indeed, in four-door saloon form, there was very little sportiness about the 15/98; it was more of a luxury saloon, and not a particularly fast one because the four-cylinder engine had a lot of bodywork to move.

That said, the smaller, open versions of the 15/98 remained relatively sprightly and fun to drive, with a top speed of over 80mph.

There is no doubt that the 15/98 moved Aston Martin forward in terms of styling and market appeal. Unfortunately, though, the Second World War brought a halt to the company's development plans and, after the cessation of hostilities, the postwar Aston Martins would be very different animals altogether.

SPECIFICATION

Engine: Four inline cylinders with overhead camshaft

Capacity: 1950cc

Bore x stroke: 78x102mm

Maximum Power: 98bhp at 5000rpm

Maximum Torque: n/a

Transmission: Four-speed manual

Suspension: Front: Rigid axle with leaf springs. Rear: Live axle with leaf springs

Length: 4000mm

Width: 1590mm

Height: 1400mm

Weight: 1150kg

Top Speed: 83mph

0-60mph: n/a

Atom
1939

THE ATOM WAS A ONE-OFF PROTOTYPE yet, as things turned out, it was one of the most important cars Aston Martin ever built. Why? Because it was after driving the Atom, that David Brown decided to buy Aston Martin in 1947, and its underpinnings went on to be the basis for the postwar DB range of production cars right up to 1958.

However, that was not the original plan. The Atom was planned as a production car and was the brainchild of Aston Martin designer, Claude Hill, and he used some revolutionary ideas. First, the car was built around a cage of square tubes (the so-called Superleggara principle that would go on to be the basis of later Aston Martins) onto which the aluminium body panels were attached.

And what a body it was! Hill's design stunned the prewar world, with its futuristic streamlined shape. The Atom was like no other car, its curvaceous lines hinted at a brave new world and its integrated front grille, low-mounted headlamps and long pointed bonnet looked powerful and aggressive. Oddly, despite the curved bodywork, all the glass on the car was flat, necessitating a split windscreen.

There was more to the Atom than just its space age appearance, though. Under the bonnet was a new four-cylinder, 2.0-litre engine designed by Hill himself (although, initially, the 15/98 engine was used). And this was linked to an exciting four-speed gearbox that was electromagnetically controlled – instead of a conventional gearlever, the driver selected gears using a small, dash-mounted controller.

The suspension was developed with the help of engineer, Gordon Armstrong, and consisted of a conventional live axle with leaf springs at the back, and independent trailing arms and coil springs up front.

It was an impressive package and one, if it had gone into production, that would have shaken up the staid motor industry of the time. Sadly, though, it was not to be, as the Second World War put paid to the plans and Aston Martin became involved in producing aircraft parts for the war effort.

However, Claude Hill didn't neglect his baby and continued to develop it in spare moments throughout the war. And then, when Aston Martin went up for sale, the by now scruffy-looking Atom was one of the company's few assets. David Brown took it home with him for a few days' driving and was so impressed, he bought the company. So if it hadn't been for the little Atom, Aston Martin – assuming it survived – would be a very different company and we wouldn't have had the DB range of cars.

SPECIFICATION

Engine: Four inline cylinders with twin SU carburettors
Capacity: 1970cc
Bore x stroke: 82.5x92mm
Maximum Power: 80bhp at 4760rpm
Maximum Torque: n/a
Transmission: Four-speed manual with electromagnetic control
Suspension: Front: Independent, trailing arms and coil springs. Rear: Live rear axle with trailing arms and leaf springs
Length: 4430mm
Width: 1540mm
Height: 1500mm
Weight: 1200kg
Top Speed: 102mph
0-60mph: n/a

2-Litre Sports ('DB1')

1948-1950

THE FIRST ASTON MARTIN PRO-duced under the directorship of David Brown was the 2-Litre Sports of 1948. Because of this, and the fact it was followed by the DB2, this rare car is often retrospectively known as the 'DB1', although it was never badged thus.

Because funds and time were tight, the 2-Litre Sports used as its basis the same tubular chassis as the prewar Atom, albeit lengthened and modified, and fitted with different suspension front and back.

The aluminium body was styled by Frank Feeley, who had previously been at Lagonda. It might not have been as radical as that of the Atom, but the shape was nonetheless modern, smooth and elegant. And, importantly, its distinctive grille would be the inspiration for all future Aston Martins, right up to the

present day. An unusual feature was a clever housing for the spare wheel within the left-hand front wing, while the rear wheel arches could be removed and replaced with flush panels to cover the tops of the wheels completely.

The car was a two-seater, but the bench seat did allow a third person to be squeezed in if required. The Sports was designed as a drop-head coupe, although a couple of examples were built with fixed roofs.

The 2-Litre Sports was powered by the 1970cc four-cylinder engine that Claude Hill had developed for the Atom, although this time it was linked to a conventional four-speed gearbox. The compact engine looked lost under that long bonnet and didn't give the car the performance it deserved but, at the time, it was the only powerplant available to the company.

A racing version of the 2-Litre Sports was also produced and became known as the 'Spa Special' because it won the legendary 24-hour race in 1948, driven by St John Horsfall and Leslie Johnson. This was great publicity for Aston Martin and did much to raise the profile of the marque around the world. Sadly, though, it was not enough to persuade many buyers in the austere postwar economy to buy a car that was more than twice the price of the contemporary Jaguar XK120, which did much the same job.

Indeed, in the event, Aston Martin only produced around 15 examples of the expensive 2-Litre Sports between 1948 and 1950, the majority being drophead coupes. It was then replaced by the more powerful and more refined DB2 with its six-cylinder engine.

SPECIFICATION

Engine: Four inline cylinders with twin SU carburettors

Capacity: 1970cc

Bore x stroke: 82.5x92mm

Maximum Power: 90bhp at 4750rpm

Maximum Torque: n/a

Transmission: Four-speed manual

Suspension: Front: Independent, trailing arms and coil springs. Rear: Live axle with coil springs

Length: 4470mm

Width: 1710mm

Height: 1410mm

Weight: 1145kg

Top Speed: 80mph

0-60mph: n/a

DB2
1950-1953

THE FIRST ASTON MARTIN TO carry a 'DB' badge was the DB2 which was first unveiled in 1950 and was promptly described as 'the most beautiful car in the world' by an enthusiastic Motor magazine.

And it truly was a wonderful-looking machine. Designer Frank Feeley created something that was way ahead of most other cars on the road in appearance and there was a hint of Italian styling in the DB2's flowing lines.

The body panels were hand-formed from lightweight 18-gauge aluminium and attached to a strong but light square-section tubular frame, which

was derived from that of the prewar Atom prototype. The bonnet and front wings were combined into one large panel that tipped forwards to give excellent access to the engine.

The engine itself was a straight-six unit designed by WO Bentley. It featured an iron block, twin overhead camshafts and had a capacity of 2580cc. Producing 105bhp at 5000rpm, it was a powerful unit for its day, and a top speed of 117mph was considered quite respectable.

SPECIFICATION

Engine: Six inline cylinders with twin overhead camshafts

Capacity: 2580cc

Bore x stroke: 78x90mm

Maximum Power: 105bhp at 5000rpm

Maximum Torque: 169Nm at 3000rpm

Transmission: Four-speed manual

Suspension: Front: Independent, trailing arms and coil springs. Rear: Live rear axle with trailing arms and coil springs

Length: 4130mm

Width: 1650mm

Height: 1360mm

Weight: 1111kg

Top Speed: 117mph

0-60mph: 11.2 seconds

The power was fed through a four-speed gearbox that was sourced, not surprisingly, from the David Brown Group and it had synchromesh on all gears.

The very early DB2s had three-piece front grilles but, on later cars, the three sections were merged into a single grille to give a cleaner design that would be aped in later Aston Martins.

The DB2 was available in coupe and drophead coupe forms, while a more powerful Vantage version followed at the end of 1950. This was also available in coupe and drophead coupe forms, and had a more powerful engine that produced 125bhp, thanks in part to larger twin SU carburettors.

Inside, the DB2 was strictly a two-seater car, with passengers enjoying a comfortable, leather-lined cockpit. Luggage space, however, was limited to a small area behind the seats. The small hatch that was accessed from the rear of the car was filled with the spare wheel.

The DB2 was an expensive car. In 1952 the coupe version cost £2724 in the UK, which was around £1000 more than the contemporary Jaguar XK120. Over its three-year production life, 411 examples of the DB2 were built, and about one-quarter of those were drophead coupes.

DB Mark III

1957-1959

THE DB2/4 MARK II WAS REPLACED by the DB Mark III, which was to be the final incarnation of the cars developed from Claude Hill's Atom chassis and with the Lagonda-based straight-six engine.

The car's name is rather confusing because you'd expect it to be called the DB3, but that name had already been used for a racecar, so the new road-going model was called DB Mark III, although it's often incorrectly referred to as the DB3.

The new car was an evolution of the

DB2/4 Mark II, but with a few small but noticeable changes to the body shape. At the front, the previously fussy grille was simplified and put in front of a new, elegantly curved bonnet. Out back, meanwhile, the tail-lights were replaced by slender vertical units. It was a simple restyle but enough to restore the elegance to the DB.

Inside, a much-needed new instrument cowl echoed the shape of the grille and gave Aston Martin a modern dashboard at long last. The useful hatchback and practical load space remained on the coupe versions.

The 3.0-litre straight-six engine had been reworked by Tadek Marek with a stiffer crankshaft, new block, new oil pump, larger valves, high-lift camshafts, a new exhaust system and much more. The result was an output of 162bhp at 5500rpm. An optional DBC engine came equipped with three Weber carburettors and was claimed to produce a heady 214bhp (just 14 cars were built with this engine). To cope with the extra power, all but the first 100 DB Mark IIIs were equipped with front Girling disc brakes instead of drums.

As before, the power went through a four-speed manual gearbox. However, in 1959 a Borg Warner automatic transmission became an option for the first time – a sign that Aston Martin was trying to widen its appeal – but only five cars were thus equipped in the end.

In its production life, a total of 551 DB Mark IIIs were built, of which 462 were coupes and 84 were drophead coupes. With its revamped engine, it was a far better car than the earlier DB2s and, as such, is much sought after today.

SPECIFICATION

Engine: Six inline cylinders with twin overhead camshafts

Capacity: 2922cc

Bore x stroke: 83x90mm

Maximum Power: 162bhp at 5000rpm

Maximum Torque: 195Nm at 3000rpm

Transmission: Four-speed manual

Suspension: Front: Independent, trailing arms and coil springs. Rear: Live rear axle with trailing arms and coil springs

Length: 4300mm

Width: 1650mm

Height: 1360mm

Weight: 1179kg

Top Speed: 120mph

0-60mph: 12.6 seconds

DB4

1958-1963

WORK BEGAN ON THE DB4 AT about the same time as the DB Mark III was being developed. The new car debuted at the 1958 London Motor Show and, in fact, the DB Mark III also continued in production for another year after.

The DB4 was essentially an all-new car. Gone was the long-serving square-tubed frame, to be replaced by a hefty sheet-steel floorpan with a tubular steel cage above, on which the hand-formed aluminium body panels were attached – a system called Superleggara. It was a strong and stiff construction, if a trifle over-engineered because of cost constraints.

The four-seater body was designed by the Italian Carrozzeria Touring company and drew inspiration from earlier DBs, but with a dash of Italian flair. In other words, it looked simply gorgeous and the DB4 remains, for many, the definitive Aston Martin.

Under that long bonnet with its pur-

poseful air-scoop lay a new 3.7-litre, six-cylinder engine designed by Tadek Marek. Unlike the previous DB engine, this one had an all-alloy construction, thus saving weight. In standard form, this engine, that looked almost as good as the car, produced 240bhp at 5500rpm, while the Vantage version, which came later, was boosted to 266bhp at 5750rpm.

With this sort of power, the DB4 became the first production car to be capable of reaching 100mph and returning to a standstill in under 30 seconds – the 0-100mph time was cited at 21 seconds, while all-round disc brakes helped on the way back to zero. And with a 0-60mph time of 9.0 seconds and a heady top speed of 140mph, here was a machine that could compete with the best of the Italian supercars of the day.

The power was fed through a four-speed manual gearbox with the option of an overdrive, which made for more comfortable high-speed cruising. A Borg-Warner three-speed automatic was also optional.

Over its production life, the DB4 was revised and updated and there are five distinct versions, which are known as Series 1 to Series 5 (some of the last ones had the cowled headlamps from the DB4 GT and looked very similar to the DB5). A convertible version was also offered from 1961.

SPECIFICATION

Engine: Six inline cylinders with twin overhead camshafts

Capacity: 3670cc

Bore x stroke: 92x92mm

Maximum Power: 240bhp at 5500rpm

Maximum Torque: 325Nm at 4250rpm

Transmission: Four-speed manual with optional overdrive, or three-speed automatic

Suspension: Front: Independent, upper and lower A-arm and coil springs. Rear: Live rear axle with Watt linkage, trailing arms and coil springs

Length: 4480mm

Width: 1680mm

Height: 1310mm

Weight: 1296kg

Top Speed: 140mph

0-60mph: 9.0 seconds

DB4 GT

1959-1963

A YEAR AFTER THE STUNNING NEW DB4 debuted, Aston Martin again wooed customers at the London Motor Show. This time with the DB4 GT. This was, though, much more than simply a more powerful incarnation with a 'GT' badge attached; it was a very different car in many ways.

The GT used the same Superleggera system as the standard DB4, with its tubular steel cage and steel floorpan under an aluminium body. However, the wheelbase was a full 130mm shorter and the car was now strictly a two-seater.

This was to improve the car's handling – especially on a racetrack – and it also served to make it lighter by about 80kg (that steel floorpan was relatively heavy compared to the body above).

The same basic body styling remained, albeit with smaller doors to suit the shortened wheelbase. At the front, though, appeared a new feature that would go on to be an Aston Martin trademark right through the 1960s – the headlamps were set back and covered with distinctive cowlings to aid aerodynamics.

The DB4 GT was powered by an uprated version of the DB4's all-alloy 3.7-litre engine. Twin sparkplugs per cylinder, triple Weber 45DCO carburettors and some other detail changes combined to boost power to no less than 302bhp at 6000rpm – an astonishing figure for its day.

The performance was no less astonishing, either. The DB4 GT, with its lighter body and more powerful engine, could shoot to 60mph in a blisteringly quick 6.4 seconds (that's still fast by today's standards) and go on to a top speed of 153mph. It's handling, too, was excellent, while uprated race-style brakes helped to cope with the extra power. In its day, the DB4 GT was pretty much unbeatable.

However, an even more powerful version, the DB4 GT Zagato appeared in 1960. This had a completely restyled body, from the Italian Zagato company, a race-style interior and a 314bhp engine. Only 19 examples of this expensive piece of exotica were built. However, in 1991, four more were built by Zagato.

SPECIFICATION

Engine: Six inline cylinders with twin overhead camshafts

Capacity: 3670cc

Bore x stroke: 92x92mm

Maximum Power: 302bhp at 6000rpm

Maximum Torque: 325Nm at 5000rpm

Transmission: Four-speed manual

Suspension: Front: Independent, upper and lower A-arm and coil springs. Rear: Live rear axle with Watt linkage, trailing arms and coil springs

Length: 4440mm

Width: 1680mm

Height: 1320mm

Weight: 1227kg

Top Speed: 153mph

0-60mph: 6.4 seconds

DB5
1963-1965

DB5 WAS AN EVOLUTION OF THE last of the DB4s that preceded it and went on to become perhaps the most famous Aston Martin of all time, after it appeared in the James Bond films Goldfinger and Thunderball in the early 1960s.

The new car was very similar in appearance to the DB4 Series 5, with the distinctive cowled headlamps that first appeared on the DB4 GT. Indeed, it was almost called the DB4 Series 6. As before, the body used a steel chassis with a unique tubular frame, on which the aluminium body panels were mounted. By making the car around 90mm longer, there was slightly more room inside, making it a more comfortable touring car. The downside was, though, that it was a heavier car.

However, it was under the bonnet

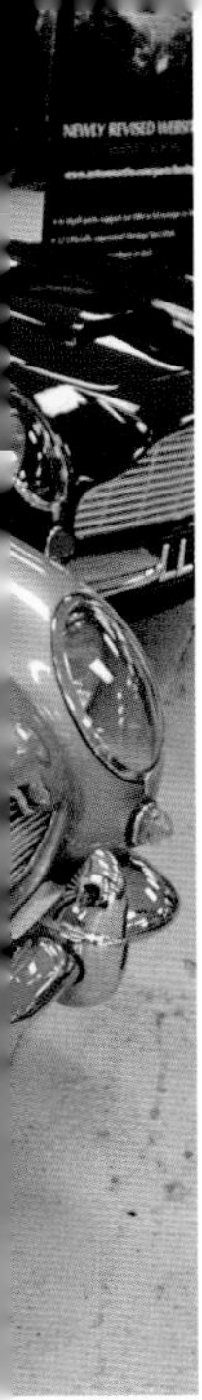

that the real changes occurred. The DB5's six-cylinder engine had an increased capacity, and was now 4.0-litres thanks to an increase in bore to 96mm. This led to a power output of 282bhp at 5500rpm in standard form. Unfortunately, though, the extra weight of the car pretty much negated the increase in power, so it wasn't until the Vantage version arrived, with its 314bhp at 5750rpm, that a real improvement in performance over the DB4 could be noticed.

As before, the standard four-speed gearbox could be supplemented with an optional overdrive. However, from 1964, the car was fitted with a new five-speed gearbox. A three-speed automatic remained an option but was rarely chosen.

Performance figures were impressive, with 60mph appearing in just 7.1 seconds and the DB5 going on to a top speed of 142mph.

Inside, the DB5 retained the distinctive instrument cowling that echoed the shape of the radiator grille, and this was filled with an array of dials. Leather and Wilton carpet ensured that the car was a comfortable and appealing place for two front passengers, plus two small ones in the back seats.

In its two-year production life, 886 DB5 coupes were built, plus 123 convertibles. There were also 12 shooting brakes, or estates, specially built to order by the Radford coachwork company.

SPECIFICATION

Engine: Six inline cylinders with twin overhead camshafts

Capacity: 3995cc

Bore x stroke: 95x92mm

Maximum Power: 282bhp at 5500rpm

Maximum Torque: 390Nm at 3850rpm

Transmission: Four-speed manual with optional overdrive (five-speed from 1964), or three-speed automatic

Suspension: Front: Independent, upper and lower A-arm and coil springs

Rear: Live rear axle with Watt linkage, trailing arms and coil springs

Length: 4570mm

Width: 1680mm

Height: 1320mm

Weight: 1466kg

Top Speed: 142mph

0-60mph: 7.1 seconds

DB6
1965-1970

ONCE AGAIN, THE DB6 WAS AN evolution of the previous model, the DB5, rather than an all-new car, although it did feature a number of changes.

Unveiled at the 1965 London Motor Show, under the skin, the DB6 moved away from the complex and expensive Superleggara construction and more towards a sheet-steel framework onto which the aluminium bodywork was attached.

That bodywork was restyled to ensure that the DB6 stood out from its predecessors. At the rear, the curved bootlid was replaced by a more modern and angular item with a neat built-in lip spoiler to aid aerodynamics. The rear side-windows, too, were reshaped with a thicker, more prominent C pillar. The front end, meanwhile, remained largely unchanged from that of the DB5, with its trademark Aston Martin grille (although a secondary grille appeared under the numberplate to feed air to the oil cooler).

The DB6 was 90mm longer than the DB5 and had a slightly higher roofline, thus improving the accommodation inside, especially for rear passengers. Apart from that and new front seats, the interior was much the same as that of the DB5.

The engine, too, remained unchanged

from the DB5 unit, being the now trusted straight-six, all-alloy 4.0-litre powerplant. The power was still 282bhp at 550rpm, although a Vantage version offered a worthwhile 325bhp. By now, the standard gearbox was a five-speed manual, while a three-speed automatic remained on the options list.

The DB6 was updated in 1969 and became the Mark II, although it was almost badged 'DB7'. This had lipped wheel arches, to accommodate wider wheels, whilst a small number were fitted with fuel injection, instead of carburettors.

SPECIFICATION

Engine: Six inline cylinders with twin overhead camshafts

Capacity: 3995cc

Bore x stroke: 95x92mm

Maximum Power: 282bhp at 5500rpm

Maximum Torque: 390Nm at 3850rpm

Transmission: Five-speed manual with optional overdrive or three-speed automatic

Suspension: Front: Independent, upper and lower A-arm and coil springs. Rear: Live rear axle with Watt linkage, trailing arms and coil springs

Length: 4620mm

Width: 1680mm

Height: 1360mm

Weight: 1474kg

Top Speed: 148mph

0-60mph: 6.1 seconds

The open-top DB6 was the first Aston Martin to carry the Volante name – the word is Italian for flying – although earlier convertibles are sometimes incorrectly referred to as such. As with the DB5, the Radford coachbuilding company made a small number of shooting brake or estate versions of the DB6.

DBS and DBS V8

1967-1972

WHEN ASTON MARTIN UNVEILED the all-new DBS at Blenheim Palace in Oxfordshire in 1967, it addressed the fact that the current DB6 was beginning to look dated – which was not surprising, considering it could trace its lineage back to the 1950s.

The DBS, on the other hand, was bang up to date, with its more angular lines, penned by William Towns, that would go on to form the mainstay of the Aston Martin line right into the 1980s. While the new car was very obviously an Aston Martin, it was larger and more aggressive than the DB6. At the front, the Aston Martin grille was cleverly reworked, to make it more integral with the bonnet line, and twin headlamps were set into the sides of the grille.

The chassis was essentially that of the DB6, albeit widened (by a noticeable 150mm) and lengthened. As ever, the bodywork was hand-formed from aluminium.

The DBS looked a mean muscle car but, unfortunately, under that huge bonnet lay the same six-cylinder engine from the DB6. In the larger car it gave adequate rather than earth-shattering performance. Aston Martin was working on a new V8 engine but it wasn't ready, which is why the six had to suffice.

By 1969, however, the new engine

was ready and was used in the DBS V8. With a capacity of 5.3 litres, twin overhead camshafts per cylinder bank and fuel injection, this beast of an engine produced 320bhp at 5000rpm and powered the DBS to 60mph in 6.0 seconds and on to a top speed of 160mph – not bad for a car that really could hold four people in comfort.

The six-cylinder variant continued to be offered alongside the V8 and, rather confusingly, went on to be badged 'Vantage' from 1972, even though that name was usually used for high-performance models. At the same time, the DBS badge was dropped from the V8-engined car and that then became known as the Aston Martin V8. This car remained in production, with only minor changes, into the 1980s.

SPECIFICATION - DBS

Engine: Six inline cylinders with twin overhead camshafts
Capacity: 3995cc
Bore x stroke: 95x92mm
Maximum Power: 282bhp at 5500rpm
Maximum Torque: 390Nm at 3850rpm
Transmission: Five-speed manual with optional overdrive or three-speed automatic
Suspension: Front: Independent, unequal wishbones and coil springs. Rear: De Dion axle with trailing arms, lever-arm dampers and coil springs
Length: 4580mm
Width: 1830mm
Height: 1330mm
Weight: 1588kg
Top Speed: 140mph
0-60mph: 7.1 seconds

SPECIFICATION - DBS V8

Engine: V8 cylinders with twin overhead camshafts
Capacity: 5340cc
Bore x stroke: 85x100mm
Maximum Power: 320bhp at 5500rpm
Maximum Torque: 542Nm at 4000rpm
Transmission: Five-speed manual with optional overdrive or three-speed automatic
Suspension: Front: Independent, unequal wishbones and coil springs.
Rear: De Dion axle with trailing arms, lever-arm dampers and coil springs
Length: 4580mm
Width: 1830mm
Height: 1330mm
Weight: 1727kg
Top Speed: 160mph
0-60mph: 6.0 seconds

Lagonda
1976-1989

THE ASTON MARTIN LAGONDA WAS unveiled in 1976 to an astonished world. There'd never been another car like it, and there never will be. It was conceived as a high-powered saloon car that would open up new markets for the company and, seeing that Aston Martin owned the Lagonda marque, it was decided to use that as a model name, rather than a brand – hence Aston Martin Lagonda.

The underpinnings were basically that of the DBS-based V8 of the day, so there was nothing particularly high-tech or revolutionary about that. However, it was the car's styling that created all the attention. The William Towns design was strikingly angular, with a long, low wedge-shaped bonnet (with a tiny Lagonda grille at the front) and there was hardly a curve to be seen.

The interior, too, was ahead of its time. Inside of traditional dials, the dashboard was equipped with space-age LED displays, touch-sensitive controls and a single-spoke steering wheel. In contrast, there were also acres of leather and wood, as befitted a luxury car.

Under that slender bonnet lay the 5.3-

litre V8 engine from the company's other cars, and this was equipped with Weber carburettors and linked to a crude and power-sapping Chrysler three-speed gearbox.

Although it was first shown in 1976, it wasn't until 1979 that the first Lagondas were delivered to eager customers. Over the years it was in production, it received a number of updates. The LED dashboard proved troublesome so in 1984 it was replaced with one that featured cathode ray tube displays, but these turned out to be just as unreliable, so vacuum fluorescent instruments were used from 1987. In the same year, the razor-sharp lines were softened slightly and the original pop-up headlamps were replaced by an array of three square lamps each side of the grille. The engine was also revised over the years, with the output reaching 300bhp.

In all, a total of 645 Lagondas were built and it proved particularly popular in the Middle East, which took about 30 percent of the total production of these expensive, hand-built status symbols. There was also a small number of long wheelbase Tickford Limousines that boasted colour televisions in the front and the back, while a Swiss company produced a shooting brake version.

The Aston Martin Lagonda was quietly dropped from the range at the end of the 1980s. It remains a unique car and very much a product of the 1970s. Some people think it's ugly and tacky, while others love the fact that it's so different from anything else on the roads. Whatever, there is no doubt that it will always remain a head-turner!

SPECIFICATION

Engine: V8 cylinders with twin overhead camshafts

Capacity: 5340cc

Bore x stroke: 85x100mm

Maximum Power: 280bhp at 5000rpm

Maximum Torque: 488Nm at 3000rpm

Transmission: Three-speed automatic

Suspension: Front: Independent, unequal wishbones and coil springs. Rear: De Dion axle with trailing arms, self-levelling dampers and coil springs

Length: 5283mm

Width: 1816mm

Height: 1302mm

Weight: 2064kg

Top Speed: 148mph

0-60mph: 7.9 seconds

V8 Vantage
1977-1989

AFTER THE DBS V8 BECAME KNOWN simply as the V8, it remained in production and a high-power variant was developed for 1977. Following the odd situation where the 'Vantage' badge was used on the entry-level six-cylinder model at the start of the 1970s, this time it reverted to its rightful place – on Aston Martin's flagship model.

The V8 Vantage used essentially the same bodyshell that dated back to the DBS of the 1960s, but was revised with new aerodynamic aids to help high-speed handling and to make the car look somewhat more modern and more aggressive. The previously open-fronted bonnet scoop became a closed power bulge in the bonnet, while the trademark Aston Martin radiator grille was blanked off and held two circular spotlights. Underneath this was a deep front spoiler with an air intake within it, while out back there was also a pronounced boot spoiler.

However, the main reason for the Vantage was to be found lurking under that purposeful bonnet bulge. The 5.3-litre V8 engine was breathed on to make it even more powerful. Indeed, Aston Martin claimed a 40 percent increase in power and a 10 percent increase in torque over the standard car's engine. This was achieved by adapting an engine that had already appeared in the Nimrod racecar. Compared to the standard V8, this unit had revised camshafts, new intake system and manifolds, larger inlet valves, four twin-barrel Weber carburettors and different spark plugs.

SPECIFICATION
Engine: V8 cylinders with twin overhead camshafts
Capacity: 5340cc
Bore x stroke: 85x100mm
Maximum Power: 380bhp at 6600rpm
Maximum Torque: 552Nm at 4000rpm
Transmission: Five-speed manual
Suspension: Front: Independent, unequal wishbones and coil springs. Rear: De Dion axle with trailing arms, lever-arm dampers and coil springs
Length: 4665mm
Width: 1890mm
Height: 1325mm
Weight: 1820kg
Top Speed: 170mph
0-60mph: 5.3 seconds

The result was a beast of an engine that, in initial form, produced a healthy 380bhp at 6000rpm and propelled the big supercar to 60mph in 5.3 seconds and on to a top speed of 170mph. The only downside, perhaps, was an average fuel consumption figure of 11 miles per gallon! The power was fed through a five-speed manual gearbox, while the suspension, brakes and wheels were all uprated accordingly.

The V8 Vantage remained in production until 1989, by which time the engine power had risen to 438bhp at 6000rpm, thanks to fuel injection and other changes, and top speed was close to 190mph. By this time, though, the design was really beginning to show its age (remember that it dated back to the DBS of the late 1960s) and very few of these large and expensive cars were built in the model's final years.

V8 Volante
1978-1989

DURING THE MID-1970S IT WAS thought that open-top cars would be outlawed in the USA on safety grounds, so many car manufacturers stopped developing them at this period, preferring to concentrate on coupes.

As it turned out, though, the feared legislation did not happen and the buyers continued to demand open-top cars – especially Americans, who were keenly buying up older Aston Martin Volantes and the like, to enjoy in the sunny climates of places like California and Florida.

Aston Martin quickly rose to the challenge and produced an open version of its large V8 model, which was aimed squarely at the US market, which took much of the production. The new model was called the V8 Volante and used essentially the same body as the coupe, albeit stiffened to make up for the lack of a solid roof and fitted with a restyled bonnet. The elegantly styled hood raised and lowered at the touch of a button, after two catches were undone at the front, using an electro-hydraulic mechanism, and was fully lined to ensure quiet and refined high-speed motoring.

The interior of the V8 Volante was similar to that of the coupe but was enhanced with burr-walnut trim for extra opulence (a feature that didn't come to the coupe until later). The rear seats remained, making it one of the few open-top cars of the time that four people could enjoy in comfort.

The Volante was also offered with the more powerful Vantage engine, and this car was known, not surprisingly perhaps, as the V8 Vantage Volante.

By the mid-1980s, Aston Martin attempted to update the lines of the V8 Volante by endowing it with front and rear spoilers and sideskirts, similar to those used on the closed Vantage. Unfortunately, though, this was not a successful look and the car was criticised for looking rather tasteless – Prince Charles, when he ordered one, sensibly asked for the bodykit to be omitted from his car.

Around 900 V8 Volantes were built during its long 11-year production run (which compares to 2658 coupes) of which many went to the USA.

SPECIFICATION

Engine: V8 cylinders with twin overhead camshafts

Capacity: 5340cc

Bore x stroke: 85x100mm

Maximum Power: 380bhp at 6600rpm

Maximum Torque: 552Nm at 4000rpm

Transmission: Five-speed manual

Suspension: Front: Independent, unequal wishbones and coil springs. Rear: De Dion axle with trailing arms, lever-arm dampers and coil springs

Length: 4585mm

Width: 1890mm

Height: 1370mm

Weight: 1791kg

Top Speed: 150mph

0-60mph: 6.3 seconds

Bulldog

1980

AFTER DESIGNER WILLIAM TOWNS shocked the motoring world with the Aston Martin Lagonda of 1976, he came back and did it all over again in 1980, with the astonishing Bulldog concept car.

It was very obvious that the Bulldog came from the same pen as the Lagonda – its low, angular wedge shape was a dead giveaway. However, the Bulldog – which stood just over one-metre tall – pushed the boundaries even further with massive, power-operated, gullwing doors, a single 60cm-long wiper blade, and a front 'bonnet' panel that dropped away to reveal an array of five headlamps. It was a striking car but took little, if any, inspiration from Aston Martin's illustrious past.

Another break with tradition was the car's layout – the engine was mid-mounted. This was – and still is – the preferred configuration for supercars but Aston Martin always preferred – and still does – to have the engine mounted at the front, driving the rear wheels. The advantage of a mid engine is that it makes the car well-balanced which can help high-speed handling.

The engine itself was a 5.3-litre V8 unit fitted with twin Garrett turbochargers and fuel injection, which was claimed to produce as much as 700bhp, although 650bhp was a more realistic output.

SPECIFICATION

Engine: V8 cylinders with twin Garrett turbochargers
Capacity: 5344cc
Bore x stroke: n/a
Maximum Power: circa 650bhp at 6000rpm
Maximum Torque: circa 670Nm at 5500rpm
Transmission: Five-speed manual
Suspension: Front: Independent with wishbones and coil springs
Rear: Independent with trailing arms and coil springs
Length: 4270mm
Width: 1918mm
Height: 1092mm
Weight: 1730kg
Top Speed: 191mph
0-60mph: 5.2 seconds

The reason for such a powerful engine was that the Bulldog was designed to break the magical 200mph barrier. The car was taken to the MIRA test ground where it was driven at a maximum speed of 191mph before unwanted lift forced the driver to back off. With further development it's likely that 200mph would have been possible

The interior of the Bulldog was just as exciting. The two-seater cockpit boasted digital displays and touch-sensitive controls, as seen in the Lagonda. In contrast, though, there was also Connolly leather, Wilton carpet and even walnut, on display in the wel l-appointed interior.

The Bulldog was a stunning machine and would have been a true super-car, if it had gone into production; at one point it was planned to produce a limited edition of about 25 cars. But that didn't happen; just the one example was built and this was sold to a private buyer soon after the 1980 launch. It was taken to the USA where it was repainted from silver and grey to metallic green, the fuel injection was replaced with Weber carburettors and other minor changes were made.

V8 Zagato

1986-1988

THE MID-1980S WAS the time of limited production supercars, with Porsche offering the 959 and Ferrari the 288 GTO. These were both high-tech cars that were, more often than not, bought by speculators rather than true enthusiasts, because there was a buoyant market for such exotica.

Aston Martin was quick to cash in on this, but didn't have the resources to compete with Porsche and Ferrari to produce a technologically advanced machine. Instead, it relied on good old-fashioned brute power and the adoption of a famous name – Zagato. This Italian styling firm had penned the Aston Martin DB4 GT Zagato in the early 1960s and this car was a sought-after collectors' item, so it made sense to milk this connection.

The new V8 Zagato was based on a shortened (by 406mm) version of the current V8's chassis. This was then clad in a rather angular and dumpy aluminium body, that was certainly distinctive but drew little on previous Aston Martins, save a stylised and squared-off front grille. The twin headlamps were set back under clear covers – a nod to the original DB4GT Zagato, perhaps.

The bonnet was punctuated by a massive bulge which was not part of the original design but proved necessary when it was decided to equip the V8 engine with 50mm Weber downdraught carburettors. The original plan was to use the standard engine from the V8 Vantage which, by this time, was fuel injected, but Aston Martin wanted to advertise the V8 Zagato as having at least 400bhp, and the only affordable way to do that was to use carburettors.

In the event, the engine was honed to such an extent that it developed no less than 432bhp at 6200rpm. Another reason for this power was that it was hoped that the car would hit the magical 300kmh mark (that's 186mph) and reach 60mph in less than five seconds. In the event, it was clocked at 299kmh, which was considered close enough! The 0-60mph dash, however, did come in as hoped, at just 4.8 seconds.

They were impressive figures for a car that lacked the turbochargers, fuel injection and even the ABS brakes which were essential requirements of the V8 Zagato's competitors.

Inside, the V8 Zagato's occupants were cosseted with leather and walnut, plus a well-equipped dashboard that was as angular as the car's exterior.

Just 52 examples of the V8 Zagato were built. However, there were also an additional 37 open-top Volante versions. As well as the folding roof, these also differed in that they had a less powerful engine with fuel injection and so didn't have the unsightly bonnet bulge.

SPECIFICATION

Engine: V8 cylinders with twin overhead camshafts
Capacity: 5340cc
Bore x stroke: 85x100mm
Maximum Power: 432bhp at 6200rpm
Maximum Torque: 535Nm at 5100rpm
Transmission: Five-speed manual
Suspension: Front: Independent wishbones and coil springs. Rear: De Dion axle with Watt linkage, trailing arms, lever-arm dampers and coil springs
Length: 4390mm
Width: 1860mm
Height: 1295mm
Weight: 1650kg
Top Speed: 185mph
0-60mph: 4.8 seconds

Virage

1988-1995

BY THE END OF THE 1980S, THE Aston Martin product range consisted of the now very dated V8 cars, which could trace their origins back to the 1960s and were looking very old-fashioned indeed. A new model was desperately needed, but there wasn't the money to invest in anything too radical.

Instead, the new car used as its base a shortened and modified Lagonda chassis onto which was mounted a stylish new body designed by John Heffernan and Ken Greenley. The new car appeared less bulky and less aggressive-looking than its predecessor and – perhaps unfortunately if you knew – was fitted with Volkswagen headlamps and rear lamps. On the whole, though, the design worked and was a successful reinterpretation of the classic Aston Martin lines for the 1980s and beyond. As before, the body was hand-made from aluminium by craftsman at the Newport Pagnell factory.

Power came from essentially the same V8 engine but one that had been thoroughly reworked by the American company, Calloway Engineering. The

most noticeable change to the 5.3-litre engine was the adoption of all-new cylinder heads with four valves per cylinder, that allowed the use of unleaded fuel while, at the same time, maintaining power and improving economy.

In its initial form, the Virage engine produced 330bhp. However, in 1992, a 6.3-litre version came out and, by 1993, this engine was producing no less than 465bhp, thus addressing earlier criticisms that the original Virage was underpowered. By this time, the car's smooth lines were joined by flared wheel arches and larger front and rear spoilers. Also, ABS was available as an option for the first time on an Aston Martin.

The Virage interior was unashamedly luxurious because, by this time, wealthy buyers wanted to be pampered and Aston Martins had become known as luxury cars rather than pure sporting machines. There was, though, among all the leather and walnut, a sprinkling of Ford switchgear and other parts, which distracted a little from the overall effect. However, the good news was that the car was quieter and more comfortable than the previous model.

The Virage was also available in open-top Volante form from 1990, albeit with a slightly less powerful engine. Oddly, this was initially planned as a two seater but, by the time it went into production, it had the same four seats as the coupe version.

Although the Virage name was dropped in 1995, the same basic body design continued up until 2000, badged simply as 'V8'.

SPECIFICATION

Engine: V8 cylinders with twin overhead camshafts

Capacity: 5340cc

Bore x stroke: 85x100mm

Maximum Power: 330bhp at 6000rpm

Maximum Torque: 474Nm at 3700rpm

Transmission: Five-speed manual or three-speed automatic

Suspension: Front: Independent, transverse unequal wishbones and coil springs

Rear: De Dion axle with trailing arms, Watts linkage and coil springs

Length: 4735mm

Width: 1854mm

Height: 1321mm

Weight: 1790kg

Top Speed: 155mph

0-60mph: 5.8 seconds

Vantage
1992-2000

THE VANTAGE WAS LAUNCHED AT the 1992 Birmingham Motor Show as Aston Martin's new flagship model. Apart from the short-lived DBS-bodied Vantage of the early 1970s, this was the first time that an Aston Martin had been named simply 'Vantage', rather than the moniker being used as an amendment of another name.

The Vantage used essentially the same chassis as the Virage, albeit substantially modified to make it lighter and to improve handling. The hand-made aluminium body also looked very similar to that of the Virage, yet Aston Martin claimed that only the roof and the door skins were carried over from that car. The rest of the bodywork was new and flared wings, front and rear, gave the Vantage a wider, more aggressive and purposeful appearance.

The front of the Vantage retained the trademark Aston Martin grille, which was actually more defined than on the Virage, while the Virage's square headlamps (which were actually Volkswagen Corrado items) were replaced by clusters of three small, square lamps hidden behind clear plastic covers. The rear lights, meanwhile, were four round units. There were also side air-vents behind the front wheels, a deep front spoiler, sideskirts and an integral rear spoiler. The overall effect was that of a supercar that certainly meant business!

And that business was lurking under the long bonnet. The trusty 5.3-litre V8 engine from the Virage was endowed with a pair of Eaton superchargers – turbocharging was considered but dismissed because of the associated problems with turbo-lag. The result was a maximum power output of no less than 550bhp at 6500rpm, combined with a torque figure of 745Nm.

Fed through a six-speed manual gearbox, this was enough to propel the big car to 60mph in a mere 4.6 seconds and on to a top speed of 186mph. This really was an astonishing motorcar! However, there was more to come in 1998, when a 600bhp version was introduced.

The Vantage had essentially the same interior as the Virage, with four seats and plenty of leather and walnut to remind occupants that they were in a very special car, indeed.

The Vantage was very much a bespoke car that was built in very small numbers. Indeed, between 1992 and 2000, just 280 examples were built, in both coupe and open-top Volante forms. The last of the line were badged 'Le Mans' and featured blanked-out radiator grilles, a larger front spoiler, cooling ducts in the bonnet and different vents in the front wings. The owner's handbook even included directions to the Le Mans circuit!

SPECIFICATION

Engine: V8 cylinders with twin overhead camshafts and twin Eaton superchargers
Capacity: 5340cc
Bore x stroke: 85x100mm
Maximum Power: 3550bhp at 6500rpm
Maximum Torque: 745Nm at 4000rpm
Transmission: Six-speed manual
Suspension: Front: Independent, transverse unequal wishbones and coil springs
Rear: De Dion axle with trailing arms, Watts linkage and coil springs
Length: 4745mm
Width: 1920kg
Height: 1330mm
Weight: 1920kg
Top Speed: 186mph
0-60mph: 4.6 seconds

DB7
1994-1999

THE FIRST ASTON MARTIN TO BE produced under Ford's ownership was the DB7, which appeared in 1994 and really was a thing of beauty. It was conceived as a spiritual successor to the DB4 and, therefore, smaller and lighter than the big V8s that preceded it. And, crucially, it would have a straight-six engine, just like the DB4, albeit a more powerful and refined powerplant. This concept of a smaller, less expensive, higher volume Aston Martin had originally been mooted by Victor Gauntlett and was instrumental in the sale of the company to Ford.

To keep costs down, the engine was, in fact, based on that previously used in the Jaguar XJ40. It was a light alloy, twin camshaft, straight-six, with a capacity of 3228cc. The cylinder head featured four valves per cylinder with Zytec electronic multi-point fuel injection, while the air needed to combust the fuel was delivered by a water-cooled Roots-type, supercharger, which was driven by a toothed belt from the camshaft.

As it was, the Jaguar connection went much deeper, much to the annoyance of some purists. The DB7's chassis was based on that of the old XJS, while the car was built in the factory at Bloxham in Oxfordshire that had been used for the XJ220 supercar.

SPECIFICATION

Engine: Six cylinders inline with twin overhead camshafts, four valves per cylinder and supercharger

Capacity: 3239cc

Bore x stroke: 91x83mm

Maximum Power: 335bhp at 5500rpm

Maximum Torque: 500Nm at 3000rpm

Transmission: Four-speed automatic or five-speed manual

Suspension: Front: Independent, double wishbones and coil springs. Rear: Independent, lower wishbones with upper halfshaft links and coil springs

Length: 4631mm

Width: 1830mm

Height: 1238mm

Weight: 1725kg

Top Speed: 165mph

0-60mph: 5.8 seconds (manual transmission)

What's more, the DB7's designer, Ian Callum, had worked on the XJ220, as well. Callum was shown a DB4 and DB6 and asked to come up with a modern interpretation of them. And that's just what he did. He ignored the larger V8 cars, feeling that they were not in the true spirit of the marque, and came up with a pure design that was immediately recognisable as an Aston Martin and had clear links with the DB4 and DB6. What the new car wasn't, though, was a pastiche or a retro car – it was strikingly modern and forward thinking in its appearance.

Inside, too, the DB7 embraced Aston Martin values. In other words, there was plenty of leather and wood on show, and the cockpit was comfortable and luxurious, with two seats in the back that were ideal for children. OK, so some of the switchgear was derived from Ford, but at least it worked properly.

The DB7 was developed on a very tight budget and in a short timescale, yet remains to this day one of the best-looking cars ever built. It relaunched Aston Martin onto the world market – it sold in no less than 29 different countries – and proved to be a practical and enjoyable sportscar with a timeless appeal.

DB7 Vantage

1999-2003

AS GOOD AS THE ORIGINAL SIX-cylinder DB7 had been, there was a demand for a more powerful and more refined powerplant. And that car came along in 1999.

The DB7 Vantage replaced the original six-cylinder model and was powered by a new V12 engine – it was the first time a V12 had been fitted in an Aston Martin.

The engine was developed by Aston Martin with the help of Ford and Cosworth. The all-alloy unit was not much heavier than the original straight-six and boasted 48 valves and a capacity of 5935cc (commonly rounded up to 6.0-litres). Visteon EEC V engine management controlled the fuel injection, ignition and diagnostic systems.

This gave a maximum power output of 420bhp – a useful 85bhp more than the old engine – and it was delivered with a silky smoothness but – and this is the crucial point – the exhaust note remained aggressive and purposeful, as you'd expect of an Aston Martin.

There was, though, much more to the Vantage than a new engine. Aston Martin had spent two years listening to customers and exhaustively testing prototypes. More than 500,000 test miles were covered in temperatures ranging from -30°C to +45°C in Europe and North America, including an accelerated high-speed durability test of 48 hours continuous running at 165mph in Southern Europe in mid-summer temperatures.

In Britain a series of pre-production models of the DB7 Vantage were subjected to continuous 30-day accelerated durability tests – each equivalent to 100,000 miles of regular driving, at speeds of up to 140mph.

The test cycles included regular passage through mud and salt baths, driving deliberately into traffic island kerbstones at 50mph and a series of fierce stop-start acceleration and brake tests. Body chassis components were tested to the limit over corrugated and ladder frame surfaces and specially engineered tracks littered with potholes and strategically placed concrete blocks.

The suspension and brakes were revised to cope with the extra power, while the transmission was upgraded to a new six-speed manual, with the option of a five-speed automatic.

The body was restyled, too, with a more aggressive front end, with larger air intakes and big round driving lights on each quarter.

The original DB7 was a great car, but the V12 Vantage made it even better. It did, though, take the concept a little away from the original roots of the DB4 and DB6, which were powered by straight-six engines.

SPECIFICATION

Engine: V12 cylinders with four overhead camshafts and four valves per cylinder

Capacity: 5935cc

Bore x stroke: 89x79.5mm

Maximum Power: 420bhp at 6000rpm

Maximum Torque: 540Nm at 5000rpm

Transmission: Five-speed automatic or six-speed manual

Suspension: Front: Independent, double wishbones and coil springs

Rear: Independent, lower wishbones with upper halfshaft links and coil springs

Length: 4666mm

Width: 1830mm

Height: 1238mm

Weight: 1780kg

Top Speed: 185mph

0-62mph: 5.0 seconds (manual transmission)

Vanquish

2001-2006

THE VANQUISH WAS ASTON Martin's first flagship car of the 21st century, hand-built at the Newport Pagnell factory and, as such, was suitably state-of-the-art.

The large, curvaceous body was designed by Ian Callum and made use of exciting new technology to ensure a strong, stiff and light structure.

The main body structure, including the floor and the front and rear bulkheads was formed from extruded aluminium sections bonded and riveted around the carbon fibre transmission tunnel. Single-piece composite inner body side sections with carbon fibre windscreen pillars were then bonded to the central structure.

At the front, a steel, aluminium and carbon fibre subframe carried the engine, transmission and front suspension. The front end incorporated deformable composite panels to provide crash protection and there was a similar

structure at the rear.

The underside of the car was completely flat to aid high-speed aerodynamics.

All the exterior panels, including the roof, bonnet, boot lid, front and rear wings and doors were produced from 'super-plastic-formed' and pressed aluminium. However, each individual panel was then tailored and bonded to the central structure by hand to ensure a perfect fit and finish.

Under that long bonnet lay essentially the same 6.0-litre V12 engine used in the DB7 Vantage, but uprated to produce no less than 460bhp and 542Nm of torque and linked to a drive-by-wire throttle system. The power went through a close-ratio, six-speed manual transmission that boasted Formula One-style finger-tip controls. These allowed clutchless gearchanges to be made in less than 250 milliseconds. Furthermore, the gearbox could be set to make fully automatic changes when desired.

All this ensured superb performance, with 62mph coming up in just five seconds and the car going on to a top speed of 190mph – the Vanquish was a true supercar.

The Vanquish had a refreshingly modern interior, with aluminium and carbon 5fibre replacing the traditional Aston Martin wood. However, there was still plenty of high-quality leather and Wilton carpet to cosset the lucky inhabitants. The car was offered with a choice of just two seats, with a luggage space behind, or four seats, with the rears being ideal for children.

SPECIFICATION

Engine: V12 cylinders with four overhead camshafts and four valves per cylinder

Capacity: 5935cc

Bore x stroke: 89x79.5mm

Maximum Power: 460bhp at 6500rpm

Maximum Torque: 542Nm at 5000rpm

Transmission: Six-speed manual with Auto Shift Manual/Select Shift Manual (ASM/SSM) electro-hydraulic control system

Suspension: Front: Independent, double wishbones and coil springs

Rear: Independent, double wishbones with upper halfshaft links and coil springs

Length: 4665mm

Width: 1923mm

Height: 1238mm

Weight: 1835kg

Top Speed: 190mph

0-62mph: 5.0 seconds

DB7 Zagato

2002-2003

ASTON MARTIN FIRST WORKED with the Italian styling company, Zagato in 1961, when the two companies produced the DB4GT Zagato. Then, in 1987 came the V8 Zagato. So, it was not altogether surprising when it was announced that the two companies would collaborate once more on an exciting new project.

That was to become the DB7 Zagato. Based, as the name suggests, on the V12-engined DB7, the new car used some of the styling cues of the original DB4GT Zagato (the 1980s version was ignored) to produce a stunning interpretation for the 21st century.

The extra-large front grille was a Zagato trademark, as were the long bonnet, chopped tail, curvaceous rear arches and 'double bubble' roofline. The bodyshell was hand-made in Italy from aluminium with a steel roof and used a shortened DB7 Vantage Volante chassis. It was assembled in the UK at Aston Martin's Bloxham plant.

The powertrain remained standard DB7 fare, with the 6.0-litre V12 engine producing 420bhp. However, because the shortened aluminium was a full 60kg lighter than the standard car, it gave the Zagato a performance advantage. This was further enhanced by revised gear and differential ratios (it was available with a six-speed manual transmission only). The brakes and suspension were also uprated to give enhanced, sportier handling.

Zagato designed unique wheels for the car, which were 18 inches in diameter and had different offsets to give the DB7 Zagato a wider track to ensure the wheels filled the wider arches.

Inside, the Zagato interior was based on that of the standard DB7, but had a trimmed luggage shelf in place of the rear seats. The door trims were revised to suit the higher waist line, while the seats were trimmed in unique quilted leather with a Zagato 'Z' on the back of each.

Just 99 examples of the DB7 Zagato were built between 2002 and 2003, and they sold for around £160,000 each. They were offered in just three standard colours; Mercury Grey, Aqua Verde and Zagato Nero, while the leather interior was Dark Chocolate aniline leather.

SPECIFICATION

Engine: V12 cylinders with four overhead camshafts and four valves per cylinder

Capacity: 5935cc

Bore x stroke: 89x79.5mm

Maximum Power: 420bhp at 6000rpm

Maximum Torque: 540Nm at 5000rpm

Transmission: Six-speed manual

Suspension: Front: Independent, double wishbones and coil springs

Rear: Independent, lower wishbones with upper halfshaft links and coil springs

Length: 4481mm

Width: 1830mm

Height: 1244mm

Weight: 1740kg

Top Speed: 190mph

0-62mph: 4.9 seconds

DB American Roadster 1

2003-2004

FOLLOWING ON FROM THE DB7 Zagato, Aston Martin and the famous Italian design company collaborated once more on another project. This was an open-top version of the Zagato – although Aston Martin was at pains to stress that it was, in fact, a model in its own right.

Indeed, it had a very different (and, it has to be said, rather clumsy) name – DB American Roadster 1, or DB AR1. This set it apart from the Zagato and made it clear that the car was designed specifically to appeal to American customers.

Despite this, it was clear that the DB AR1 was very much based on the coupe Zagato and shared the same styling, front and back. The main difference, of course, was the lack of a roof. Indeed, the car had no form of roof whatsoever, not even a folding soft-top – making it a roadster in the truest sense of the word, and only suitable for fair climes, such as California.

Like the Zagato, the bodyshell was hand-made in Italy and was mainly aluminium. Behind the seats were two distinctive humps, which echoed the 'double bubble' roof of the coupe.

Unlike the Zagato, though, the DB AR1 was equipped with an uprated version of the 6.0-litre V12 engine that produced no less than 435bhp at 6000rpm – up a worthwhile 15bhp from the standard 420bhp unit, while torque increased from 540Nm to 556Nm at 5000rpm. The exhaust system, meanwhile, had bypass valves in the rear silencers to give a sportier note.

The power went through an AP twin-plate racing clutch and a six-speed manual gearbox with revised ratios. To suit the target American market, a five-speed automatic gearbox was available as an option.

Brakes were upgraded, too, with racing-style grooved 355mm (front) and 330mm (rear) Brembo discs and Pagid RS 42-1 front pads. An uprated brake booster unit – as used on the V12 Vanquish – assisted in providing the driver with progressive braking and a firmer and more consistent pedal feel.

Zagato designed unique, lightweight alloy wheels for the DB AR1 that were 19 inches in diameter and had revised offsets to suit the wider wheel arches.

The DB AR1 interior was based on that of the standard DB7 but was uniquely trimmed in Bridge of Weir leather.

Just 99 examples of the DB AR1 were built in 2003 to 2004 and they were eagerly snapped up by collectors, hoping for a good long-term investment.

SPECIFICATION

Engine: V12 cylinders with four overhead camshafts and four valves per cylinder

Capacity: 5935cc

Bore x stroke: 89x79.5mm

Maximum Power: 435bhp at 6000rpm

Maximum Torque: 556Nm at 5000rpm

Transmission: Six-speed manual or five-speed automatic

Suspension: Front: Independent, double wishbones and coil springs

Rear: Independent, lower wishbones with upper halfshaft links and coil springs

Length: 4481mm

Width: 1830mm

Height: 1229mm

Weight: 1730kg

Top Speed: 190mph

0-62mph: 4.8 seconds

DB7 GT

2003-2004

THE DB7 REALLY WENT OUT WITH a bang before it was replaced with the all-new DB9. The DB7 GT was the last of the line and the most powerful DB7 ever, with its V12 tweaked to produce a full 435bhp (up from the standard 420bhp).

However, the increase in power was only part of the story. Aston Martin made the GT a more sporty car to drive than the standard DB7. Not only was there more mid-range torque from the uprated engine, the GT also had a revised final-drive ratio with limited-slip differential, active sports exhaust, a quick-shift gearchange and a racing twin-plate clutch (on manual transmission cars).

To make the DB7 really stand out, it received some subtle styling changes that, not only made the car look more

sporty and purposeful, also improved its aerodynamics, especially at high speed.

Under the car, the undertray was revised to improve downforce, as were the wheel arch liners. Combined with a lip spoiler on the bootlid, these reduced lift by almost 50 percent – useful when you're heading towards the car's top speed of 185mph.

SPECIFICATION

Engine: V12 cylinders with four overhead camshafts and four valves per cylinder
Capacity: 5935cc
Bore x stroke: 89x79.5mm
Maximum Power: 435bhp at 6000rpm
Maximum Torque: 556Nm at 5000rpm
Transmission: Five-speed automatic or six-speed manual
Suspension: Front: Independent, double wishbones and coil springs
Rear: Independent, lower wishbones with upper halfshaft links and coil springs
Length: 4692mm
Width: 1830mm
Height: 1243mm
Weight: 1800kg
Top Speed: 185mph
0-62mph: 5.0 seconds (manual transmission)

The stylists at Aston Martin also added a pair of distinctive vents in the GT's bonnet. These fed air to the engine and also helped to reduce under-bonnet temperatures. There was also a new mesh front grille with a subtle 'GT' badge on it.

Also unique to the DB7 GT were 18-inch light-alloy wheels with five spokes that allowed a good view of the massive, grooved brake discs with their four-piston calipers. The wheels were shod with high-performance, low-profile Bridgestone tyres to provide optimum levels of performance and grip. Meanwhile, electronic traction control went even further in helping to keep the GT on the road, but without distracting from the fun of driving the car.

Despite the extra sportiness, the GT was no stripped out racecar. Inside, the passengers were treated to a full leather interior, electrically controlled and heated front seats, climate control, six-speaker Kenwood stereo system with CD autochanger, carbon fibre trim and much more.

By the time the GT arrived, the DB7 was a full 10 years old and beginning to show its age. It was, though, a great finale to a great car.

DB9

2003

THE DB7 WAS A GREAT SUCCESS BUT, by the start of the 21st century, it was beginning to show its age. The Vanquish had shown the way forward with its space-age construction and this was the inspiration behind the DB7's replacement, the DB9.

A quick note on names is in order here. The obvious badge for the new car would have been DB8, but it was thought that this would cause confusion with the new 'baby' Aston Martin, the V8 Vantage, so the new V12-engined car was named DB9.

The DB9's lines were quite obviously an evolution of what came before it, yet more aggressive than the DB7 with more than a hint of Vanquish in the mix.

Construction-wise, the DB9 was streets ahead of the conventional DB7. It had an immensely stiff, bonded aluminium frame onto which the body panels were attached, using high-tech adhesives. The bonnet, roof and rear wings were aluminium, while the front wings and bootlid were composite. The entire structure was 25 percent lighter than the DB7 bodyshell.

The DB9 was powered by essentially the same V12 engine as used in the DB7 Vantage, but it was fettled to increase the maximum power to 450bhp and the torque to 570Nm.

To ensure a 50:50 weight distribution, the front-mounted engine was linked to a rear-mounted gearbox. Two transmissions were offered; a conventional six-speed manual or a six-speed automatic. The latter was revolutionary in that it used a 'shift by wire' gearchange instead of the usual selector lever; a system of buttons were used to select Park, Reverse, Drive or Neutral. It also gave the option of Formula One-style manual shifts using paddle controls on the steering column.

The DB9 had a plush and well-appointed cabin in the best Aston Martin traditions. As well as the usual leather, there was also an abundance of aluminium which was most evident in the dash. The instruments had three-dimensional aluminium faces which were 'floodlit' rather than backlit, to make them look extra-special at night. Unusually, the rev-counter ran anti-clockwise and did not have a conventional red line because the rev limit varied (depending on the engine's mileage, how recently the engine had been started and the ambient temperature). Instead, a red warning symbol came on when maximum revs were reached.

Wood is traditional on Aston Martins, but for the DB9 the designers steered clear of small amounts of 'glued on' veneer trim and opted instead for a large, solid, piece in the centre of the dash top and, optionally, in the door trims as well.

The DB9 was produced in coupe and open-top Volante styles.

SPECIFICATION

Engine: V12 cylinders with four overhead camshafts and four valves per cylinder

Capacity: 5935cc

Bore x stroke: 89x79.5mm

Maximum Power: 450bhp at 6000rpm

Maximum Torque: 570Nm at 5000rpm

Transmission: Six-speed manual or six-speed automatic

Suspension: Front: Independent, double wishbones and coil springs

Rear: Independent, double wishbones with longitudinal control arms and coil springs

Length: 4710mm

Width: 1875mm

Height: 1270mm

Weight: 1760kg

Top Speed: 186mph

0-60mph: 4.9 seconds

Vanquish S

2004

THE ORIGINAL VANQUISH WAS AN impressive machine, but Aston Martin made it even better with the S version, which was unveiled at the Paris Motor Show in 2004.

The updated car was an evolution of the original Vanquish and had the same revolutionary extruded aluminium and carbon fibre body structure, which was hand-assembled at Aston Martin's Newport Pagnell factory. It was, though, subtly updated. At the front, there was a more rounded radiator grille and a deeper front spoiler to aid the aerodynamics. At the back of the car, meanwhile, the bootlid was redesigned with a larger lip spoiler and an integral central brake light.

The 6.0-litre V12 engine also received attention. A new cylinder head design, revised mapping, new injectors and other changes increased the maximum power by no less than 60bhp to give

520bhp at 7000rpm, while peak torque was raised to 577Nm at 5800rpm.

The power went through the same six-speed manual transmission with paddle shifters, but the final drive ratio gearing was shortened to give better mid-range performance; for instance, the 50-70mph acceleration time (in top gear) was improved by almost two seconds.

SPECIFICATION

Engine: V12 cylinders with four overhead camshafts and four valves per cylinder
Capacity: 5935cc
Bore x stroke: 89x79.5mm
Maximum Power: 520bhp at 7000rpm
Maximum Torque: 5477Nm at 5800rpm
Transmission: Six-speed manual with Auto Shift Manual/Select Shift Manual (ASM/SSM) electro-hydraulic control system
Suspension: Front: Independent, double wishbones and coil springs
Rear: Independent, double wishbones with upper halfshaft links and coil springs
Length: 4665mm
Width: 1923mm
Height: 1238mm
Weight: 1875kg
Top Speed: 200+mph
0-62mph: 4.8 seconds

To cope with the extra power, the Vanquish S received revised brakes with larger discs and six-piston front calipers, while the suspension was lowered and treated to uprated springs and dampers. The steering, too, was changed to make its response 20 percent faster.

All this combined to ensure that the Vanquish S was an even faster and more exciting car to drive. Indeed, at the time of its launch, it was the fastest production car Aston Martin had ever built.

However, it was also a luxury car, as you'd expect of an Aston Martin. The interior remained essentially the same as the original Vanquish, but received some detail updates, and was a sumptuous place to be, with aluminium, leather, Wilton carpet and Alcantara in abundance. As before, buyers could choose between two seats with luggage space behind, or two small seats for children in the back.

Because the cars were hand-built to order, customers could specify whatever interior and exterior colours they wished, and you could even have stainless steel plates engraved with your name attached to the door sills.

V8 Vantage
2005

THE V8 VANTAGE WAS FIRST HINTED at in 2003, when Aston Martin showed the AMV8 Vantage concept car at the Detroit Motor Show. The reaction to the idea of a 'baby' Aston Martin was phenomenal and so the car went into production two years later as the V8 Vantage.

The name was, perhaps, a little confusing, because the Vantage badge was traditionally used for high-performance variants, whereas the V8 Vantage was an entry-level Aston Martin.

Not to worry, though, because it was still a superb car; smaller and more agile than its big brothers, the DB9 and Vanquish, yet with the traditional Aston Martin attributes of style and quality, mixed with a good dose of high-tech.

Underneath the stunningly good-looking body lay a bonded aluminium frame (derived from that of the DB) onto which the aluminium, steel and composite panels were attached. The result was a light, stiff and strong structure.

The body was finished off with state-of-the-art lighting, with LED (light emitting diode) indicators, side repeaters, rear and brake lights. High-power xenon headlamps were an option.

As its name suggests, the V8 Vantage was powered by an all-new 4.3-litre V8 engine made entirely of aluminium and capable of producing a healthy 380bhp and 417Nm of torque. The engine was mounted well back under the bonnet to help give an even weight distribution to aid handling. This was helped by mounting the gearbox at the rear of the car and linking it to the engine with a carbon fibre propshaft. The gearbox itself was either a six-speed manual or a six-speed automatic with manual changes via Formula One-style paddle shifters.

Unlike the DB9, the V8 Vantage was strictly a two-seater car, while an opening rear hatch allowed a good amount of luggage to be carried, making it a practical long-distance tourer.

And the interior made it a car you'd be happy to be in for long periods. It combined traditional, hand-trimmed leather and aluminium with modern ergonomics and style, and high-tech options such as satellite navigation and a Bluetooth telephone link.

The V8 Vantage was followed by an open-top Roadster version.

SPECIFICATION

Engine: V8 cylinders with four overhead camshafts and four valves per cylinder

Capacity: 4300cc

Bore x stroke: 89x86mm

Maximum Power: 460bhp at 6500rpm

Maximum Torque: 542Nm at 5000rpm

Transmission: Six-speed manual or six-speed automatic with manual shifts

Suspension: Front: Independent, double wishbones and coil springs

Rear: Independent, double wishbones and coil springs

Length: 4380mm

Width: 1865mm

Height: 1255mm

Weight: 1630kg

Top Speed: 175mph

0-62mph: 5.0 seconds

Rapide Concept

2006

AT THE 2006 DETROIT MOTOR SHOW in the USA, Aston Martin unveiled an exciting concept car. And to everyone's surprise, it was a four-door, high-performance sports saloon, in much the same manner as the Lagonda of the 1970s.

The Rapide, as the car was called, was obviously based on the DB9 coupe, but was stretched to improve accommodation for rear passengers and to make room for the extra doors. Aston Martin was able to achieve this relatively simply by virtue of its VH (Vertical/Horizontal) architecture that formed the backbone of the DB9. The extruded aluminium construction could be modified in both length and width, providing a myriad of packaging options, and the bonded structure was mated with the aluminium and composite bodywork.

The result was an impressive machine that had real presence while, at the same time, being slick and elegant. The Rapide concept car had different headlamps to the DB9 – more angular projector items – and a novel transparent roof that could be made opaque at the touch of a button.

Inside, the dashboard was based on that of the DB9 but with a new centre console, dials based on Swiss watches, and different trim finishes. Rear passengers were treated to extra legroom, a DVD player and even access to the satellite navigation system because, said Aston Martin, it was vital that both driver and passengers should be involved in route planning. The front seats, meanwhile, could lie flat so you could catch forty winks during a long, cross-continental journey.

At the back of the car was a lifting rear hatch that gave access to the useful luggage area. On the show car, this was equipped with a chess board, pack of cards and a champagne chiller! On a more practical note, Aston Martin claimed that there was room for three sets of golf clubs, or up to four pairs of skis.

Up front, meanwhile, the Rapide was powered by the same V12 engine as the DB9, but uprated to 480bhp and mated to a Touchtronic automatic gearbox with fingertip manual control when required. To counter the power, the car was the first Aston Martin to be equipped with carbon brakes and calipers.

At the time the Rapide was shown, Aston Martin insisted it would remain a concept car. However, later in 2006, it was announced that a production version would follow by 2009.

SPECIFICATION

Engine: V12 cylinders with four overhead camshafts and four valves per cylinder

Capacity: 5935cc

Bore x stroke: 89x79.5mm

Maximum Power: 480bhp at 6000rpm

Maximum Torque: 570Nm at 5000rpm

Transmission: Six-speed automatic

Suspension: Front: Independent, double wishbones and coil springs

Rear: Independent, double wishbones with longitudinal control arms and coil springs

Length: 4980mm

Width: 1915mm

Height: 1358mm

Weight: 1920kg

Top Speed: 185mph (estimated)

0-62mph: 5.0 seconds (estimated)

DBS
2007

THE 2006 JAMES BOND FILM CASINO Royale featured a new Aston Martin – the DBS. At the time, the company gave very little away about the new car, although it was very obviously a tuned version of the DB9.

The car in the film featured a new front spoiler, sideskirts and rear valance,

and air vents in the bonnet, to give a more aggressive appearance than the DB9. Although few details were available at the time of writing, it is likely that some of the bodywork would be carbon fibre to keep the weight down. The interior, too, appeared to be lightweight, with no rear seats and Alcantara and aluminium trim.

The DBS had the same V12 engine as the DB9 but tuned (possibly with superchargers) to produce in excess of 500bhp. Ceramic brakes were a possibility, too.

The DBS was due to go into production at the end of 2007.

SPECIFICATION

Engine: V12 cylinders with four overhead camshafts and four valves per cylinder

Capacity: 5935cc

Bore x stroke: 89x79.5mm

Maximum Power: 500bhp (estimated)

Maximum Torque: 600Nm (estimated)

Transmission: Six-speed manual

Suspension: Front: Independent, double wishbones and coil springs

Rear: Independent, double wishbones with longitudinal control arms and coil springs

Length: 4710mm (estimated)

Width: 1875mm (estimated)

Height: 1270mm (estimated)

Weight: n/a

Top Speed: 190mph (estimated)

0-62mph: 4.6 seconds (estimated)

Chapter 4

James Bond and Aston Martin

THINK ASTON MARTIN AND IT'S hard not to think of the 007 spy, James Bond. However, in the first Ian Fleming novel, Casino Royale, published in 1953, Bond actually drove a 1933 Bentley convertible with a 4.5-litre supercharged engine, not an Aston Martin. This was, according to the story, Bond's own personal car, which he'd owned since before the Second World War. This Bentley was then destroyed during a car chase in the next book, Moonraker, and replaced by a more modern 1953 Bentley Mark VI. Then, in the novels Thunderball and On Her Majesty's Secret Service, Bond drove a Bentley Mark II Continental which, again, was supercharged, so it was obvious that the spy enjoyed fast British cars.

Bond first drove an Aston Martin in the novel Goldfinger, published in 1959. In this book, Fleming gave his hero a DB Mark III to drive (although he incorrectly called it a DBIII, which was actually a racing car) and described it as having front and rear lights that could change colour, reinforced bumpers, a Colt .45 pistol hidden in a compartment under the driver's seat, and a homing device.

However, by the time the film of the same name came along in 1964, the

DB5 was the current model and so this was the car used by the screen Bond, although the two silver ones supplied by Aston Martin for use in the film were, in fact, almost identical-looking DB4 Mark 5s.

The car driven by actor Sean Connery was 'modified' by Q Branch with a range of special options, including twin Browning machine guns hidden behind the front sidelights, oil slick dispenser, smoke screen, extendable front and rear overriders for ramming, extendable bulletproof steel barrier behind the rear window, revolving cutters in the wheel hubs, passenger ejector seat and revolving numberplates. A generation of schoolboys enjoyed playing with the detailed Corgi model of the car. The same DB5 was used again by Sean Connery in Thunderball in 1965.

The 1967 film On Her Majesty's Secret Service featured a metallic green Aston Martin DBS, driven by George Lazenby as James Bond. However, the car didn't appear much in the film and the only 'extra' shown was a hidden compartment in the glovebox for a sniper's rifle. The DBS also appeared very briefly in the background of a scene in the next film, Diamonds Are Forever, when workers at Q Branch could be seen lowering missiles into its bonnet.

James Bond then flirted with Lotuses for a while before returning to Aston Martin for The Living Daylights in 1987. Timothy Dalton played Bond in that film and he drove a

▲The Vanquish, from the James Bond film Die Another Day, on display during the 2002 British International Motorshow

charcoal-grey V8 Vantage Volante endowed with extendable side skis, retractable spikes in the tyres, missiles, lasers in the wheel hubs, signal-intercepting smart radio, head-up display and rocket propulsion. Later in the film it was 'winterised' with a hardtop and essentially became a coupe. The car could also be set to self-destruct.

Bond then drove BMWs in subsequent films, basically because the German company was willing to pay handsomely to have its products shown.

Early in the 1995 film Golden Eye, Bond, played by Pierce Brosnan (who, incidentally, owned a Vanquish in real life), was seen driving an Aston Martin DB5, the implication being that it was his own personal car. It was, though, equipped with a refrigerator in the centre armrest that held (of course) a bottle of champagne and two glasses, and there was a communication system that included a fax machine. The same car appeared again briefly in Tomorrow Never Dies in 1997.

Interestingly, for the next film, The World is Not Enough, Bond was filmed driving a DB5 to M16's Scottish headquarters but the scene was not used in the final cut. There was, though, a brief 'thermal satellite' image at the end of the movie showing the Aston Martin in Istanbul.

The 2002 film Die Another Day featured an Aston Martin V12, which Q called the 'Vanish' on account of its adaptive camouflage that could make the car all but invisible at the touch of a button! This Aston Martin was driven by actor Pierce Brosnan and also featured a passenger ejector seat, front-firing rockets, bonnet-mounted target-seeking guns and spike-producing tyres.

In the 2006 film Casino Royale, James Bond was played by Daniel Craig. Early on in the story he won a now classic Aston Martin DB5 in a game of poker. Later, though, he drove a Q Branch-prepared Aston Martin DBS V12 – a car that wasn't even on sale to the public at the time. The only gadgets shown in the car were a secret compartment for a Walther P99 pistol and an emergency medical kit which Bond handily used to save his own life! The car later flipped over and crashed – a stunt that proved very difficult to execute on account of the car's low centre of gravity and excellent handling.

Over the years Aston Martin has become synonymous with James Bond and there is no doubt that the films have been of tremendous benefit in promoting the marque worldwide.

BELOW The two stars of Die Another Day - Aston Martin and Pierce Brosnan

Chapter 5

Things you didn't know about Aston Martin

1. The original 1969 version of The Italian Job featured a silver DB4 convertible, driven by Michael Caine's character, Charlie Crook. Sadly, the car was destroyed when it was pushed over a cliff. However, rather than waste the genuine Aston Martin, the filmmakers mocked up a Lancia to look like the DB4.

2. Actor Rowan Atkinson is an Aston Martin enthusiast and owns several, including a V8 and a DB7 which he drove in the film Johnny English. Atkinson received a driving ban for speeding in the V8, which has the numberplate 'COM 1C'.

3. Prince Charles was given an Aston Martin as a 21st birthday present from his mother, the Queen. Since then, he's become very fond of the cars and has owned several. Charles famously told off his wife, Diana, when she sat on the bonnet of one of his Aston Martins. He's also been a frequent visitor to the factory.

4. James Bond actor, Roger Moore, also drove an Aston Martin – a DBS – in the 1970s television series, The Persuaders! and also a DB5 in the 1981 film, The Cannonball Run.

5. An Aston Martin DB5 is the slowest car on the Power Laps list of the Top Gear television programme.

6. The Vanquish S features a sound system developed by the renowned Scottish hi-fi company, Linn, that boasts 13 speakers.

7. Aston Martin was not the first connection with cars for the David Brown company. Between 1908 and 1915, the Huddersfield company produced the Valveless Car, so called because the two-cylinder engine didn't use valves.

8. A model Aston Martin can be seen on the lap of a ragdoll on the cover of the Beatles album, Sgt Pepper's Lonely Heart Club Band. This is said to be a reference to rumours that Paul McCartney had been killed in an Aston Martin.

9. In 2006, Aston Martin opened a dealership in Russia for the first time, under the name 'Aston Martin Moscow'.

10. An Aston Martin branded mobile phone was produced by Nokia in 2006. The Nokia 8800 Aston Martin Edition had the marque's famous logo etched onto its stainless steel casing and cost £800 plus VAT.

11. Aston Martin Heritage Restoration can retrofit air-conditioning to older models and hide the controls to maintain the period look of the cockpit.

12. Australian pop star, Kylie Minogue, recorded a song called Aston Martin (Let's Go), which included the memorable lyrics "In my Aston Martin (oh oh ooh oh!), we might get started) (oh oh ooh oh!), In my Aston Martin you can call me darling (oh oh ooh oh!)...

13. The Aston Martin Owners' Club was formed in England in 1935 and now has branches around the world.

14. A memorial to Aston Martin's founder, Lionel Martin, was erected at the top of Aston Hill in Buckingham in 1997.

15. In the early 1970s, Ogle Design produced an unusual car based on the DBS V8 of the day. It featured a glassfibre bodyshell with an all-glass upper section. At the back was a stainless-steel with 22 holes in through which the rear lights shone; the harder the driver braked, the more lights came on. Its looks were not a success, but the Ogle was faster than the standard DBS on account of being lighter.

STRATTON MOTOR COMPANY
AUTHORISED DISTRIBUTOR

The pictures in this book were provided courtesy of the following:

Cover photo by Nick Dimbleby for Aston Martin

GLYN-COCH CRAFT CENTRE
Pwll Trap, St Clears
Carmathenshire SA33
01994 231867
www.glyn-coch.com

MICHAEL BAILIE – PHOTOGRAPHER
www.michaelbailie.com

BY KIND PERMISSION OF OCTANE MAGAZINE
www.octane-magazine.com

TIM COTTINGHAM
www.astonmartin.com

GETTY IMAGES
101 Bayham Street, London NW1 0AG

LMF 386